GAY CROW

WHAT PEOPLE ARE SAYING ABOUT GAY CROW:

"A page-turner...so much insight...a wonderful story."
— Gary O'Neil

"Gripping...a really important story and one worth telling."
— Sandip Roy

*"Unputdownable...truly amazing and unique...
a lot of guts and courage."*
— Pramod Mahajan

"The whole human condition captured in one incredible life."
— Leonard Lane

*"Much more than a well-written story...
it offers inspiration, hope, and courage."*
— Michael Konefal

"I couldn't put it down. Can't wait for the movie!"
— Tony Angov

"Absolutely heartwarming and inspiring."
— MaxPaul Franklin

"Brilliant! The man, the struggle, the story...all brilliant!"
— Amy Miller

"Truth is stranger than fiction. To say that the author has overcome the most seemingly insurmountable of odds and has lived nothing short of an astounding life would be a gross understatement.

"Just when you think the indignities, the considerable suffering that Vishwas goes through could not get worse, your senses are assaulted with something even more grim, even more sorrowful. But through it all, the Gay Crow keeps rising phoenix-like, a veritable cat with nine lives, the gay man brilliant enough to have never had to eat crow.

"Written in a crisp conversational style with lucid prose, this heart-felt memoir never falls short of being a page-turner. A testament to human resilience, it will open your eyes to what a person is truly capable of. Above all, it will restore your faith in humanity."

— **Ninad Jog**

GAY CROW

A MEMOIR

VISHWAS PETHE

ISBN-13: 978-0-578-94129-5 (Paperback)

Developmental editing by Max J. Miller

Front cover image by Abhijit Kalan.

Back cover image painted by Vishwas Pethe

Book design by Mario Lampic

Layout and typesetting by Mario Lampic

Copy editing by Diedre Hammond

Printed by Amazon, Inc., in the United States of America.

First printing edition 2021.

www.GayCrow.com

To Joe Hennessy
for being my life force,
and to Mark Yapelli
for encouraging me
to write this memoir

आनंदी कावळा

एका राज्यात एक कावळा असतो. नेहमी आनंदी, हसत! कुठल्याच प्रकारचे दु:ख, कष्ट त्याच्या चेह-यावरचा आनंद हिरावून घेवू शकत नसतात. एकदा त्या राज्याच्या राजाला ही बातमी कळते. त्याला खूप आश्चर्य वाटते, हे अशक्य आहे, त्याचे मन खात्री देते. मग तो आपल्या शिपायांना त्या कावळ्याला पकडून आणण्याची आज्ञा देतो. कैदेत ठेवल्यावर कसा आनंदी राहील पठ्ठया! राजा मनोमन आपल्या विचारावर खूश होतो. कावळ्याला कैद करून महीना लोटतो तरी तो हसतच!

राजा बेचैन होतो. "प्रधानजी, त्या कावळ्याला दु:खी करण्यासाठी काय करता येईल?"

"महाराज, आपण त्याला काट्यात टाकुया" प्रधान तत्परतेने उपाय सुचवतो.

लगेच राजाच्या आदेशाप्रमाणे शिपाई त्याला काट्यात टाकतात. तिथेही हा आपला आनंदाने शीळ घालतोय.

"महाराज, आपण त्याला तापलेल्या तव्यावर टाकुया" राणी दुसरा मार्ग सुचवते.

दुस-या दिवशी त्याला तापलेल्या तव्यावर टाकले जाते, पण कितीही चटके बसले तरी त्याच्या चेह-यावरचे हसू काही मावळत नाही.

"ते काही नाही महाराज, आपण त्याला ऊकळत्या तेलात टाकू" सेनापती पुढची शिक्षा सुचवतात.

दुस-या दिवशी भल्यामोठ्या कढईत तेल ऊकळवून त्यात त्याला टाकले जाते. तरीही कावळा हसतोच आहे.

शेवटी राजा हर मानून त्या कावळ्याला सोडून देतो आणि प्रजेला सांगतो आपण पण या कावळ्या सारखे कुठल्याही परीस्थीतीत हसत व आनंदी राहुया.

Gay Crow: A Fable

There once was a kingdom ruled by a very unhappy king. One day, a visitor told the king about a gay (happy) crow who lived in the forest. Intrigued, the king sent soldiers to find the happy crow and throw him in jail. The soldiers reported to the king that, even in jail, the crow remained happy.

"Cast him into the thorns," the king commanded.

But, even among the thorns, the crow sang and was happy.

"Put him in a hot oven," the king ordered. "And, if that doesn't make him unhappy, boil him in hot oil!" Nothing seemed to turn the crow from his happiness.

Finally, the king relented and let the crow go free. The king declared to the people, "Let us all be like this gay crow and find happiness in whatever circumstances we find ourselves."

Foreword

I've never met anyone like Vishwas before. When I met him, he was suicidal, but not really depressed. He often had thoughts of killing himself, but was always pleasant, joyful, and had an electric smile. He's quite literally a genius, but he had a hard time comprehending why his suicidality hurts those who care about him. He laughed at the absurdity of society's prohibitions on him choosing to end his own life.

Vishwas should be dead. He should have died thirty years ago, and he should have died seventeen years ago, and he should have died thirteen years ago. He could have died when he had his stroke five years ago. If he had died when HIV was a death sentence in 1986, or when he had non-Hodgkin's lymphoma in 2001, or when he was damn near out of T-cells in 2004, there would have been many mourners at his funeral, and people who loved him would have been hurting. They would have asked, "Why?" They would have missed him. If he succumbs to another stroke or dies from another ailment, or, hell, if he's hit by a bus in 2020, or 2025, or 2040, people will be hurting just the same. I'm never more aware of mortality and the fact that death is a part of life, and that loved ones hurt and then move on in their own way, as I am when I'm talking with Vishwas.

When I first met Vishwas, he told me he had decided he should die and would have killed himself if not for his husband's insistence he keep trying to live. He asked me to help him find a reason not to kill himself. I've certainly talked to a lot of people who think about killing themselves, but I don't think anyone's ever quite asked me for this. In so many words, he said, "I have no reason to live, but my husband is making me try, so can you give me some reasons to live?" If this sounds scary and baffling, that's because it is.

But I decided to trust the process. The process that my mentors have told me to believe in, and the process that I've told my own mentees to believe in. I have faith in the idea that, if I allow myself to join another person, if I allow that person to open himself to me, that eventually we'll figure something out together that will allow them to feel better.

Being a therapist provides a conflict that I assumed I would have resolved by now, but that I'm realizing is likely eternal: I am asked to help people, to fix people, to mend people, to enhance their lives, and to keep them here. But everything I've ever learned about being a therapist, from the most important psychological minds to mentors and colleagues who I trust, has taught me that there's not that much therapists can really do.

So, with Vishwas, I was initially asked to figure out a way to keep him alive, to help him find a reason to live. All I was able to do was to give him my ear, give him my empathy, allow him to feel connected, and help him think through questions that he already knew the answers to on the inside. He knew it was helpful to see me, that it gave him a rare "pleasure" in his frustrating life, but he certainly did not think (nor did I) that there was any magnificent wisdom I could impart to ease his pain. But, nevertheless, he seemed to improve. He seemed to improve in concert with the construction of our relationship.

I remain hopeful that he'll keep trying, keep engaging, and keep arduously struggling through tasks that are easy for me and I don't have to think about. He has led such a remarkable life that I regularly encouraged him to share his story with others. I'm so delighted that he has taken up the challenge and I'm honored that he chose to present his story in a condensed account of our time together. This memoir provides proof that life is not yet done with Vishwas, this matchless Gay Crow.

—Carl, Psychologist

Introduction

I've gained a deep appreciation for the work of a skilled psychologist, but the first time I saw a therapist, I was already sixty-two and all I knew of therapists came from movies and television shows. In popular media, most characters seeking the support of a therapist are either depressed, anxious, angry, or frustrated with some aspect of life. I was none of those.

If life has taught me anything, it's that my circumstances and challenges don't determine my happiness. I've camped out on death's doorstep six times in the past thirty years since being diagnosed with AIDS in 1986. For two full decades between my diagnosis and the appearance of antiretroviral medications in 2006, I continuously lived with a life expectancy of less than one year.

Ten years after my T-cell count finally reached healthy levels, I had a massive stroke that affected the left side of my brain. I had to relearn how to use my right arm and leg, and I struggled to speak clearly. My mental abilities were significantly impaired. Five months later, I had a fall injuring my left arm, twisting my jaw, and displacing all the teeth. My stroke recovery stopped. I endured the therapies for six more months.

When I had partially recovered, I woke up one day and said to myself, "I think I'm ready to go." It wasn't that I was depressed or unhappy. I simply had a sense that my life was complete. I felt that I had accomplished everything I had ever desired.

That morning when I went into the kitchen, Joe Hennessy, my husband and partner for thirty years, was sitting there having his breakfast. I kissed him on the forehead. He warmly looked at me and asked how I was feeling.

I took a deep breath and said, "I am ready to leave this life behind." Joe inquisitively cocked his head to one side. Joe has loved me through all of this. In his own way of expressing affection and support, he asked me a few questions just to better understand what I was thinking and how I was feeling.

We talked about it for a bit and then he asked me if I would be willing to see a therapist just to get a second opinion on whether this was really what I wanted or if there was anything else going on. I assured Joe that I didn't need to see a therapist. "I'm not sad," I told him.

He persisted and I agreed to see someone. I found Carl through an Internet search, and I made an appointment.

Later, I would learn that my clever husband (who is also a lawyer) knew that therapists have their own version of the Hippocratic Oath and are legally and ethically prohibited from encouraging a client's wish to end their own life.

Initially, I thought I would see the therapist just once or twice to satisfy my husband's request and perhaps give myself a little reassurance that I was doing the right thing in ending my own life.

It's been two years since I began seeing Carl. Over the course of our weekly meetings, I recounted every aspect of my life and journey. I don't know how many days that life will keep me on this planet, but I have gained such a profound appreciation for life over these past few years that I wanted to share my story. I've created this memoir in the form of a greatly condensed version of the conversations between Carl and me. I invite you to eavesdrop as I share my life journey with my therapist.

One

Good to meet you, Vishwas. What brings you here today?

I've been recovering from a stroke that I had in January 2016. I was diagnosed with AIDS in 1986, and for about twenty years, I lived with a life expectancy of less than one year. Then in 2006, I had one combination of medicines that worked for me and my viral load became undetectable. I had ten years of peaceful life after that. You could say, I've been through a lot health-wise.

The thing is, I've never let any of that stop me from being happy and doing the things I've wanted to do in life. I've been very fortunate to have a good career, a wonderful husband, and a great life.

The stroke did a number on me. The left half of my brain is dead, my right arm and leg are partially disabled, and my speech is garbled. Since I began recovering from my stroke, I just started thinking that I've lived a full life and I feel like I'm ready to go.

Do you mean ready to die? Are you telling me you are thinking about suicide?

Yes. I'm not sad or depressed. I just don't think there's anything left to keep me here. I'm just ready for my life to be over.

So, what are you hoping to get out of our time together?

When I told my husband, Joe, that I was ready to go, he asked if I would be willing to see a therapist and look for a second opinion about this and I agreed to do that.

Vishwas, I must inform you that the ethical requirements of my profession require me to do everything in my power to keep you alive. Knowing that I'm obliged to encourage you to live, do you still want to work with me? And if so, what do you hope to accomplish with me?

I just don't feel like I have a reason to keep living. Maybe you can help me find a reason. I am hoping you can help me find a new "zest of life."

That's a tall order. Tell me more about yourself and your life. How long have you and Joe been together?

Thirty years.

How do you think Joe feels about what you've shared with me?

I think he's worried that I'm unhappy. But I'm really not. I've always been a happy person. Even since childhood.

Joe says that he doesn't want me to go. He wants me to stay with him, but he also says he always wants to support me and my desires.

He just wants me to get advice from a mental health professional. I should mention: I've already had appointments with two other therapists.

How did it go with the other therapists?

Not well. I didn't feel I could connect with them and they didn't seem to be able to help me in the way I wanted. I saw one therapist for only one session and saw the other therapist twice. One of them suggested that to handle my stress, I should stand in the shower and let the water run in my face. Seriously.

Oh, my. Well, in my view, psychotherapy is all about building a relationship, and that requires authenticity. We won't get anywhere meaningful if we are not completely honest with each other. So, I want to ask you, have you made any specific plans about how you would end your life?

Not really. I've thought about it a bit, but I haven't made any plans.

I'm glad to hear that. Vishwas, I can offer you a safe, friendly space for you to sort through your own thoughts and feelings so that you can be comfortable and confident with your own choices. How does that sound?

I already feel comfortable talking with you. I had a sense when I saw your picture online that we would get along well.

That's great. I have one request for you. Will you agree to tell me if you have any specific thoughts about ending your life?

Yes. I don't think I'm a typical patient for a therapist. I'm not depressed or troubled about my life.

I already sense that, and perhaps I'm not a typical therapist. Modern psychotherapy tends to organize itself like the medical profession around treating disease. I don't see my work like that. In my view, there is a lack of intimacy in our relationships and families in our culture. A good therapist can fill that gap.

I like that. It makes sense. So, how does this work? Do you just ask me questions?

Let's approach it like a new friendship. We can both ask questions and we'll get to know one another that way.

That sounds good.

I'm curious, Vishwas, about your religious or spiritual beliefs and how that plays into your thoughts about ending your life.

Well, I'm currently not religious at all. There was a time when I believed in a super being. I pursued what that exactly meant for a long time. Then at one point, something happened and I became atheist.

Were you raised in a religious household?

I was raised in a religious culture. In India, there are many different roads to follow in the spiritual quest.

I grew up in a building adjacent to the now-famous Siddhivinayak Temple. It was a very small temple with a separate Hanuman temple attached to it. Our building was called the "Siddhivinayak Housing Society." There was no separation between our building and the temple. All the kids played in the temple yard. I always felt that being so close to the temple gave me special insights into the divine.

My grandmother used to tell me to go to the temple every Tuesday (the day of Ganesh) and pray to Lord Ganesh and ask for what I wanted. Then I learned that God is everywhere and I couldn't understand why we needed to go to the temple to meet God.

I also learned God is all-knowing, so I didn't see a reason for me to tell God what I wanted to happen. Obviously, my little brain was not going to know what is the right thing that needs to happen to make the world function well. So, I never prayed for specific things such as getting good grades.

How old were you at the time?

Perhaps eight or nine.

That's quite insightful for that age. Or any age, for that matter.

I saw that people pray for certain things. Sometimes, they come true and then they say, "God answered my prayer." Sometimes, they don't and they say, "God knows the best and he did it this way because there is a higher purpose." So, I didn't see a point in praying except to register my trust in God. So, my prayers from my earliest memories have always been, "Let the right thing happen."

Amazing. I wonder if you were aware of your exceptional insight at that age.

I was always very curious. From an early age, I've always wanted to understand how things work. Later when I was in college in the early seventies, I started to explore the usual existential questions: "Who am I?", "Why am I here?", "What is around me?", "Why is this here?", "Who controls it?" Being at Banaras Hindu University (BHU) in Varanasi on the banks of Ganga put me in the right frame of mind to contemplate these questions. At times, I would go alone to the Birla Mandir on campus and wait for an answer. My mind used to go blank and no new thoughts or revelations would come in.

Curiosity was always the main driver of my spiritual quest. Many people seek happiness or peace. Happiness was never my concern. I had no difficulty being happy. I was always good at looking at the bright side of things or remembering the good and forgetting the bad.

So, you see yourself as an optimist? The "glass is half full" sort of guy?

It's not just optimism. I feel that I am happier because I focus on and remember the happier aspects of life. My uncle told me a story when I was a boy. It's a well-known fable in India called "Gay Crow." This crow is "gay" in the sense of happiness. So here, it would be called "Happy Crow," ha-ha.

The story goes something like...There once was a kingdom ruled by a very unhappy king. One day, a visitor told the king about a happy crow who lived in the forest. The king sent soldiers to find the happy crow and throw him in jail. The soldiers reported back to the king that, even in jail, the crow remained happy. "Cast him into the thorns," the king commanded. But, even among the thorns, the crow sang and was happy. "Put him in a hot oven," the king ordered, "And if that doesn't make him unhappy, boil him in hot oil!" Nothing seemed to turn the crow from his happiness. Finally, the king relented and let the crow go free. The king declared to the people, "Let us all be like this gay crow and find happiness in whatever circumstances we find ourselves."

My uncle said I was very much like the Gay Crow, and he encouraged me to stay this way. "Stay happy." He didn't know about the gay part, ha-ha.

How has this "Gay Crow" quality shown up in your life?

I have a dear friend, Hirve, who I've known since college. He recently reminded me of a time we had difficulty getting home. I couldn't remember it as he described it. He told me we were traveling home late at night from a concert near Churchgate and we took the Western Rail train back to IIT (Indian Institute of Technology). But when we got to the end of the train, the last bus for the final leg of our journey had already left. So, we got back on the train and rode it all the way back to catch the Central Railway. We rode that train to Kanjurmarg and walked uphill through the trees to IIT. He said it was a difficult trip.

Once he reminded me of the event, I remembered it completely differently. I remember the concert had been magnificent and we were traveling the whole evening in the glow of this wonderful performance of "Shyam Sundara" by the late Kishori Amonkar. I remember he and I had a delightful conversation, talking about the concert and so many things. I had forgotten all about missing the bus and walking through the trees. I only remembered how sweet it was to spend this time with Hirve.

And that is how you see yourself...happy no matter what?

Not as much since my stroke, but I think it's how I've gotten through everything I've been through in life. I believe that everyone has a percentage of happiness and a percentage of unhappiness. Some are 70 percent happy and 30 percent unhappy. They find things to be happy about (70 percent) and things to be unhappy about (30 percent). They try to justify things to be happy or unhappy about in those percentages, no matter what the situation is.

Seems like a very healthy way to think about happiness.

This is just my theory based on my observation. I may be wrong. In that scenario, I am 90 to 95 percent happy and 5 to 10 percent unhappy.

So, it makes sense that your spiritual pursuits were more to satisfy your curiosity than a quest for happiness and peace of mind.

Happiness and peace of mind were not my goal, but I was very curious. I learned about Hindu mythology, scriptures, philosophies, yoga, and other material through books, discussions, or observations. These offered answers to my questions, but they didn't seem complete. Occasionally, I would hear sadhus and swamis preach about the "truth." Then I observed how they led their own lives and realized how *bhondu* (that is, hypocritical) they are. I wrote one of my poems about this.

You write poetry?

I wrote poems during my college years about my observations.

Do you still have them? I'd enjoy hearing what you wrote.

Yes, I have them. I'll bring them in next time. May I ask you a question?

Yes, of course. As I said, we can both ask questions like two friends getting to know each other.

Are you gay?

No, I'm straight. I'm married to a woman.

That's probably good. I've heard that people sometimes have fantasies about having sex with their therapist, so that solves that problem for me.

How so?

I generally don't have fantasies about straight men who I know. But, when I showed Joe your picture, we both agreed you are very attractive.

Well, thank you. Now, you grew up at a time when the world was not gay-friendly and I imagine your Indian culture was not gay-friendly at the time. Was that difficult for you?

It's not really that my culture was anti-gay. It was just like gay didn't exist there. Nobody talked about it. My earliest memories of sexual awareness go back to the age of ten or eleven. I had an older male cousin who used to tell me about the private parts of girls and how they give birth to children. I found out later that these stories were anatomically incorrect. But, when he used to describe these to me, I used to feel a rush of excitement, not toward the female anatomy but toward my cousin himself. At times, we used to explore each other's bodies also, and I found this quite arousing.

I had similar clandestine interactions with another cousin. The extended family gatherings provided lots of opportunities for us kids to sleep together. During these occasions, my cousin told me all about masturbation and ejaculation. I found both concepts very hard to believe. During my eleventh year, I tried to masturbate several times, usually in the latrine, with an erection but no ejaculation. One night, my cousin and I were sleeping on the terrace, with other kids. Everyone else was asleep when he started to play with me. We did some mutual masturbation and he ejaculated. I was so amazed to see this white stuff come out instead of urine.

Another such night, when I was twelve, my cousin successfully jerked me off to ejaculation. Right after I came, I had intense pain in my prostate region. This scared me. I was sure that I had broken the reproductive mechanism and it wasn't going to work again. The pain later subsided. A few days after that, I was able to masturbate on my own and come with no pain.

Once when I was thirteen, I was playing with a neighborhood kid. He wanted me to show him my penis in exchange for seeing his. He was three years younger and more aggressive than me.

This was his idea. We went to his home and took off our pants and looked at each other. Then he suggested that I take his penis in my mouth. I found the suggestion ridiculous. We kids used to use a phrase, "Take mine in your mouth." It was our version of saying, "No way, José." Despite my reservations and disgust at the suggestion, I tried to take his penis in my mouth when we heard a knock on the door. His mother came in and I could tell by the look on her face that she knew that we were doing something nasty. I left immediately.

I don't know what my friend told his mother, but soon she came over and asked to speak to my mother. I was terrified. After the two mothers had their private conversation, my mother asked me what had happened. I told her that we showed our penises to each other. My mother said, "Knowing this woman, she is going to make a big fuss over this and will probably tell everyone." She told me to stay away from this kid for a while. I didn't like the kid anyway. I spent the next few months in fear and embarrassment.

It's quite normal for boys to sexually experiment with one another. Even straight boys do this. The difference between gay boys and straight boys typically shows up in their fantasies. Straight boys tend to fantasize about girls even when they're playing with boys.

My embarrassment wasn't about being gay. I didn't know I was gay at the time. It was because I had done something that I was not supposed to do. I occasionally masturbated, but I do not remember any sexual fantasies attached to them. As I grew older, I started feeling an attraction toward my uncles and some older men in the neighborhood. I never felt any kind of attraction toward girls. When my schoolmates lustfully talked about girls, I thought that they were either blowing smoke or being "bad" boys.

My attraction toward men felt so natural to me that I never thought there was anything wrong with me. I knew that other boys liked girls. Talking about girls in "that way" was considered bad behavior in my upbringing. So, I never commented on girls. I was a "good" boy and I didn't say sexual things about girls. Nor did I speak about boys. I didn't have to lie. I just kept my attraction toward men to myself. I knew that my friends would not understand it.

Let's pick up on this next time. And please bring in some of your poems and share them with me.

Thank you. See you next Friday.

Two

I see you brought your poetry with you.

I did. I originally wrote these poems in Marathi. It was during my college years. But I'll translate them for you. The poem that I was telling you about was one I called "Hypocrite." It sums up how I felt about the sadhus and swamis.

> *You give false advice about doing good, yet you are in the dark.*
> *You have not experienced happiness, nor have you known sorrow.*
> *How long will you go around with this false claim of being a sage?*

How old were you when you wrote this?

It was during college, so I was about twenty-one years old. At that age, I still had a sort of quest for truth. As this quest was brewing in the background of my unconscious mind, sometimes I would suddenly feel detached from the things going on around me. This would last for just a moment and then things would go back to normal. I would try to recapture that feeling of detachment, but I never would get it back by conscious effort.

Sometimes, those of us who are very analytical have some difficulty processing our emotional responses to things. I was thinking about your Gay Crow story. There can be a dark side to having a persistently positive outlook. Your poem says something like, "You haven't experienced happiness nor sorrow." Do you think you have experienced the sorrow of all that you have been through?

I'm not sure what you mean.

You've experienced quite a bit of loss. Most recently with your stroke. Do you feel that you have experienced the sorrow of all that loss?

It has been very difficult. I lost half of my brain and had to learn to walk and speak all over again. I try to be the Gay Crow about everything, and this stroke has been the greatest challenge in that regard. I just read an article that got me thinking about how things might have been. The title was "Black Boy Scores Higher on IQ Test Than Bill Gates & Albert Einstein." The boy's IQ is 162. Mine is 167. It made me wonder, *Where does it put me on the scale?* I had never thought of this. But it got me thinking, *I wonder where I would be if not for the HIV I got in my twenties?*

I can see that there is sadness in that for you.

16

I don't know if I would even pass the Mensa test anymore since my stroke. I took the test and I've been a Mensa member since 1983 when they determined my IQ was 167. But I just can't dwell on that. Being the Gay Crow has served me well. I want to focus on the positive.

Do you still participate in Mensa?

I went to some of their lunch meetings. But, I found that, in the meeting, everyone wanted to impress others that he or she is so smart. So, everyone was talking and no one was listening. So, I stopped going to the meetings.

Did these spiritual pursuits lead anywhere when you were in college, writing this poetry?

Sometimes, things seemed to come together when I was studying for my masters of technology at Bombay (Mumbai) IIT. I stayed in the hostel at IIT toward the north end of Bombay and I was working on my research project in artificial intelligence at Tata Institute of Fundamental Research (TIFR) at the very southern tip of Bombay. Also, I was taking music lessons from Ramkrishna Patwardhan in Vile Parle, which was halfway between IIT and my family's home in Worli. I traveled between these four places every day by bus and train. It gave me a lot of idle time to do nothing but think and observe.

Occasionally, I would glimpse a momentary insight, but it would quickly turn back into the question itself. That's when I wrote this other poem titled "The Moment of Realization" ("जाणिवेचा क्षण" in Marathi).

> *Sometimes it seems like I'm someone else. 'This is not me,' says someone other than me. I realize that's what I want. But I call myself "me," and I miss the moment of truth.*
>
> *Sometimes he calls me from inside myself. "Leave yourself and come to me," he says. I know that's what I want. But I check myself for validation, and I miss the moment of truth.*
>
> *Sometimes I search for him. I look for him until I get dizzy. I give up. I try to enjoy life as it is, and I miss the moment of truth.*

That's beautiful. Profoundly insightful.

It didn't always feel that way to me. Often, I found life and truth to be quite perplexing. I had accepted that I am part of the Brahma. In Hinduism, Brahma is the name of the creator god, but Brahma also represents the entire creation.

Interesting. Brahma refers both to the creator god and to the entire creation itself. And you are a part of the Brahma?

Exactly. I had read that I am Brahma, but I still felt separate from it. If I was Brahma and I had created this universe, then why was

I trapped in the world myself? I expressed this paradox in a poem called, "The Mess."

> *When I started to build the universe, even the concept of time didn't exist.*
>
> *From then on I started building the atoms and molecules and giving the dimensions. From these I created the world, the sun, the moon, and the universe for the real soul to be in. I created life and death, the attraction, and the repellant, all with a set of guiding science.*
>
> *I had left an escape route out of this, but somehow I can't find it.*
> *Why did I create this mess? I cannot get hold of this anymore.*

Wow. That really captures the human condition. We feel at times limitless like a god and yet trapped like an animal in a cage.

That's it. See, you're a poet, too!

Hmm. So, you were asking some very interesting questions back in your college years. And did you find any answers?

I wasn't getting any specific answers to my questions, but everything seemed to be converging into a direction that I had read about in the Vedas (ancient Indian scriptures). My path wasn't Bhakti yoga since it needed too much faith without questioning. I tried meditation and mantra, but didn't get anywhere. My path wasn't Kriya yoga or Raja yoga because they were too hard and took too long.

My path was more like Dhyana yoga, well suited for a computer engineer. (Dhyana means "knowledge.") I was looking for an answer in science by understanding the world around me. I had read that, no matter how much I searched, it was going to end in nothingness (which is नेती नेती in Marathi). This is my poem with that title ("Nothingness"):

> *How long should I live through cycles of life and death?*
> *How long should I experience happiness and sorrow?*
> *How much do I split the atoms?*
> *How much do I expand the universe?*
> *How much do I expand the knowledge?*
> *How much do I expand the limits of time and dimension?*
> *When I know that ultimately the answer is nothingness.*
> *Nothingness, nothingness, nothingness.*

At the risk of sounding like a therapist, how did you feel about that realization?

Ha-ha. "Nothingness" in Hinduism isn't like meaninglessness or hopelessness. Nothingness is more a void of everything. It's a hard concept to describe until you experience it yourself.

It's more like an awakening to how things actually are in reality. I have another poem that gets at this called "Realization." In

Marathi, the word *moksha* (मोक्ष) means "realization." I saw people around me looking for the final solution or the ultimate answer. It's this same idea. People look for answers in many places. It reminds me of the song "Looking for Love in All the Wrong Places." Here's my poem, "Realization:"

My mind, which tries to find the meaning in the unknown,
the one who tries to draw in the trigonometry,
the one who tries to find the emptiness in music,
the one who finds energy in fossils while ignoring the
energy in the universes,
the one who is trying to find the realization in worldly things,

Would someone explain that freedom is in the mind of
the one who is already free?

Did you feel like you lost your spiritual bearings in college?

After this experience, I was neutral. I had always thought that God was one, but different people called it by different names (such as Allah, Brahma, Yahweh) and had different stories about his existence. That's what I believed based on my knowledge about other religions based on what I saw in Hindi movies.

The three main religions (Christianity, Islam, and Judaism) consisted of 56 percent of the world population. They each think that their God is the only true deity and the rest are bogus.

This started my new search for the "realization." My main profession kept me busy. And, coming to a new country and a new (gay) lifestyle kept my mind busy, but I attempted to find the "truth" where I could. For years, I went on retreats such as the Hindu Self Realization Fellowship and other spiritual practices. I was aware that this process should bring me to realization someday, but it never did. Being in a relationship with a Catholic priest (Joe) helped me understand his point of view. But my search continued.

Many years later in 2001, I developed non-Hodgkin's lymphoma. In one of the treatments at home, I had an IV and Joe was monitoring when I went into a trance. I said to Joe, "I am having a spiritual experience. Please do not disturb me." In the experience, I saw myself as a bucket of water reflecting the sun. There were other buckets of water having the same reflection. But we were separate. Demonstrating that God is one but also that individuals have a reflection of the same god. This experience was similar to a story I had heard thru Swami Tadatmananda.

I didn't think of it afterward. But it left a permanent mark on my belief in God. From then on, I understood that there was no God and my quest had vanished. If my "spiritual experience" had anything to do with it, I don't know.

And is that how you still look at it today?

Sometime much later, I was having tea with friends. They asked me about my experience and all I could tell them was, "I had a question about God and now I don't. I know that God does not exist. The only thing is science. The concept of God is implanted in the human mind when we are very young and then we spend the rest of time searching for it."

Do you still consider yourself a Hindu?

Yes. Hinduism doesn't require belief in the existence of God. In my culture, it is quite normal for the husband not to believe in God and for his wife to be pious. Or the other way around. And they are still considered Hindus.

Of course. Beliefs are only one aspect of culture, along with art, food, poetry, music, and so much more.

Art and music were very important to me as well. I mentioned that I studied Indian classical music under Ramkrishna Patwardhan in Vile Parle. He was a disciple of Pandit Bhimsen Joshi. I got to meet Panditji several times. Once I even accompanied Panditji on tanpura in the background on stage at one of his concerts at Ravindra Natya Mandir in Prabhadevi. It was the high point of my existence. After the concert, I didn't remember anything about it except that my mind had gone blank and the music was filling some void in me. I left with a feeling of elation that lasted for days.

For a fleeting moment, I imagined pursuing a career in music rather than engineering. My vocal abilities were quite bad though.

Studying under Patwardhan was an excuse to learn about music and become a कानसेन, not a तानसेन (trained ears but not trained voice). I was better suited for engineering, but I gained a deeper appreciation for music.

When I was young, I was quite a good artist as well. Until the point came when a choice had to be made. Children who showed promise in technical areas went into technical classes to learn about woodworking, machines, and metal work. My parents decided to put me there and it meant that I no longer had access to art classes.

I was very upset and cried. I told my parents that I loved art and wanted to continue in art. My father said to me, "Art you can always do in your own time, but you have to have a profession. Technical classes will get you prepared for a good career." That was the first time I cried because of pain caused to me emotionally. I remember crying three other times in my whole life, when my mother passed away, when my first partner passed away, and when Joe went to Germany.

From that day I decided, in a huff, that I will never do any art again. I kept that promise until I was in college at BHU. There, a friend of mine, Ramu, who was an artist, was doing someone's portrait. I was waiting for him to finish so we could go for dinner. Seeing my impatience he said, "You also draw a portrait," and he gave me a pencil and paper. That's when I put my promise aside and did the portrait. It turned out to be so good. From then on, I used to go with Ramu for drawing trips.

I'm curious how being Hindu affected your sexual development. Last time, you talked about sexual experimentation with your cousins and how that left you embarrassed. Was it difficult for you to explore your sexuality back in India?

I did have one gay relationship in India before I came to America. I met a man named Jimmy Irani at a bus station. We kept looking at each other, and eventually, he started a conversation with me, which led to my first sexual encounter. I had made that kind of visual connection with other guys from time to time, but there was never any opportunity to hook up.

Why was that?

Most single people live with their families in India, so you have no place to go. Jimmy had his own place, which was quite unusual. We went to his place and had sex. I quickly felt I was in love with him. In hind sight, it was the sex, but at the time it felt like love, a feeling I never had before.

Eventually, I brought him into our home. My mother didn't understand what was going on because he was much older than me and he was Farsi whereas my family was Hindu. My mother just said, "I don't know why, but I don't have a good feeling about him." I think she noticed his eyes were red because he had been drinking. Also, he was forty-two and I was twenty-two at the time.

I didn't press the issue with my family, but I kept visiting Jimmy at his home. I was always traveling between home, school, my research work, and my music classes. I always found a way to go and visit him. It was tricky to coordinate back then because we didn't have cell phones like we do today and we had to plan everything carefully.

I thought about Jimmy all the time. I was always scheming how we would meet again. He told me how he came to India from Pakistan during the partition. He told me stories of that time that were really horrific.

But, he also told me about his time in England and how he used to go to the bars. Jimmy had been in England when he was young. He told me about the bars and how gay people meet there. He told me that he used to drink screwdrivers and dance at the bars. This was the first I learned of the gay "scene." So, that was very interesting to me.

Within a few months of meeting Jimmy, I got a chance to come to the United States. My first thought was that I was in love and I didn't want to leave Jimmy. I told him I would just say no to the offer and I'll just stay in Bombay. But he encouraged me to pursue the opportunity in America.

When I came to the States, I quickly discovered the gay bars and met other gay men. It was like a whole new world for me. For the first few months, I was still remembering Jimmy as a lover and I was writing to him. I began to share with him how wonderful this all was to meet other gay men and go to the bars.

Suddenly, Jimmy felt that I betrayed him, and soon, he stopped communicating with me. Jimmy was the first gay man I introduced to my family. And, it would be quite a while before I came out again to my family. It just affirmed that my belief that my "gayness" will not be understood by regular folks.

So, it was really when you came to the US that you came out?

Yes.

Let's pick up with that next week.

Three

Good afternoon, Vishwas.

Good afternoon. What would you like to ask me today?

How are you feeling this week? Are you still having thoughts about ending your life?

I've been thinking lately that I don't really want to die right now or in the near future, but I don't want to deal with things getting worse either.

What don't you want to get worse? Are you talking about pain?

Generally, I don't cope with pain very well. And most of the time, I feel okay. Everything is more difficult since my stroke. I see so many doctors and Joe takes me to all my appointments. I just don't want to get trapped in the medical system as my faculties deteriorate.

I can imagine that can be very difficult and frustrating.

As I get worse and become more dependent, I don't want to lose my ability to choose to live or die. I want to be able to die in my own way. When I am feeling good about life, having my close friends by my side, describing the good times we had, saying goodbye to them, and then ending the life I had. Wouldn't you want to die this way rather than on a hospital bed in agony?

I understand your preference there. So, these thoughts aren't so much about your present condition. You are more concerned about your independence and autonomy at some point in the future. Is that accurate?

Yes. Most of the time, things are good right now. I'm still able to enjoy the company of my friends and Joe. I am doing okay in the grand scheme of things. I know I have so much to be happy for. But sometimes, it can be difficult to focus on this in the moments when I am miserable.

Most people struggle to regulate their emotional responses in certain situations. But I suspect for you this causes particular distress.

Why do you suspect that?

It's very important to you to stay positive and focus on the good things. You're the Gay Crow, right?

Not so much lately.

I suspect that gets closer to the heart of the problem for you. Maybe we should try some cognitive-behavioral strategies to

help you feel more powerful and in control in those situations that you describe as miserable. Then you will be empowered to focus on the good and be happy.

Okay. How would this work?

Throughout your day, I'd like you to make note of how you are feeling. Pay attention to what may have contributed to your state of mind or your mood. And especially if you have thoughts about ending your life, make a note of what may have prompted these thoughts. Just paying attention to your thoughts can empower you, but we can also develop specific strategies to deal with the thoughts that you want to modify.

So, I just write down my thoughts in a notebook?

Yes. Then we will talk about this more next week.

Okay. I'll do it.

Good. By the way, I came across some tables at Dupont Circle on the weekend and they were displaying literature for gay youth in DC. Have you ever heard of an organization called Smyle?

No, I don't believe I have.

They have programs to help young people with coming out and dealing with family and other issues. I thought of you and

maybe this could be something that could bring some "zest" to your life by helping these kids. The guy gave me his card and I told him I would pass it on to you. He said he would be happy to hear from you.

I appreciate that. Thank you for thinking of me. I will reach out to them. Maybe in a few months. I'm still very conscious of my ability to speak properly since my stroke.

I was thinking about that and I wonder if it would be helpful if I record a session and transcribe it for you. Maybe that will reassure you about your speaking and being understood.

That would be very helpful. If you think you can understand me. I didn't think my speech was understandable enough for you to do that. Thank you.

Last week, you were telling me that you had a brief relationship with a man in India before you moved to the States. Tell me about coming to America.

When I was in college, I had no interest in going abroad. I was fortunate to attend the top-rated engineering school in India and there were many opportunities at the time in India in my field of electronics and electrical engineering.

As part of the routine of graduate school, I took only one campus interview with Tata Burroughs Limited (TBL). I didn't take the interview too seriously since I had told my guide that I would do the doctorate degree under him.

Just a few weeks after I met and fell in love with Jimmy, TBL contacted me and offered me a job. In two months after starting this job, I was selected to go to the USA for a project. Because of my new relationship, I really wasn't inclined to accept their offer, but Jimmy said, "You should go ahead. It will be a good experience for you." I decided to take the job.

Initially, the company planned to train us for six weeks, but within two weeks, an assignment came up. So, they pulled me and two other guys out and sent us to Harrisburg, Pennsylvania. It was quite a shock for me. I had imagined the United States would be like New York City, but it was a small town with greenery and natural beauty.

Soon after I arrived, I started searching for gay people. After searching through the phone book for things like "gay" and "men," I found a description of a massage parlor for men. One evening, I borrowed the car from my housemates and went to see this place. I knocked on the door and a woman answered it. I immediately felt awkward and embarrassed. I left the premises immediately. But eventually, I found a gay bar.

I met a lot of guys at gay bars, took weekend trips to Philadelphia and other cities, and had a great time discovering the gay lifestyle. Jimmy stopped communicating with me, and eventually, I fell in love again with a guy named Ed. I knew that my company would move me again, but I let myself fall in love in spite of that. A few months later, Ed moved to Washington, DC.

One of my fellow students from India, Rajen, came to the US before I did. We were in Electronics class together and he wanted to go to America for a master's program. I saw him taking different tests and filling out the forms. And right after we graduated, he found out that he was accepted to University of New York, Stonybrook (SUNY) on Long Island. I had no interest at that time in coming to America and I thought I'll probably never see him again.

Now I was in Harrisburg, not too far from New York City, so I got in touch with Rajen and told him I would make a trip to visit him on a Saturday. But, I decided to enjoy the New York gay scene on the way and I took a bus up there on Friday afternoon. I went to some bar on Christopher Street. Then, I went to a gay bathhouse and met a nice guy and we spent the night together.

The next day, I took the LIRR train to Stonybrook to see Rajen. He was happy to show me around and tell me about life in America. He said, "This evening, I will show you New York City." We went to many different places and ended up in Greenwich Village. While we were crossing a street, I saw the guy I had spent the night with. Of all the people in New York, he spotted me and hugged me casually and said, "So nice to see you again." I was embarrassed.

I guess you hadn't come out to Rajen?

34

No, and I realized that now I *had* to come out to him. But, I decided to come out to my mother first. So, I closed my eyes and imagined that I was flying to Bombay to see my mother and come out to her. Then I opened my eyes and came out to Rajen. He was surprised, but he was cool about it.

Hmm. Did you eventually return home to India after your project in Harrisburg completed?

Yes. Over the course of one year, I did two projects in Harrisburg. When the second project ended, the company brought me back home. I thought that was the end of my travels and cherished my time in the USA.

When I returned home, I went on a vacation in Kokan, a mountainous region along the western edge of Maharashtra, south of Bombay. In the middle of my vacation, my boss at TBL called to tell me they had a new project for me in Australia.

So, you moved to Australia? What year was this?

Yes, it was late 1980. I did a benchmark project for a bank in Australia. We worked and lived in Sydney and Melbourne.

I didn't know anyone outside of work there, so I had to go out and find gay people on my own. One evening, I went to a "dirty" bookstore and I saw two men walking together. I followed them to an unmarked gay bar. After that, I met many more gay people.

I had a ball, but I kept my sexual interests totally hidden from coworkers.

Did you make any gay friends in the bars there?

Yes. I made a couple friends. I met a renowned Australian gay comic and we became good friends. He wrote two long letters to me. I kept those. But suddenly out of nowhere, I came across him. He has become a famous comic in Australia. I wrote to him after forty years. I sent copies of the letters to him. But after a couple of emails back and forth, he lost interest and then I didn't hear from him.

But I wasn't in Australia very long. About three months after I got there, I got a telex that a job had come up in Memphis, Tennessee, and I was the only person who could do the job (to write a new operating system).

I met a whole new bunch of gay guys in Memphis. I was alone at that time, so I had no inhibitions, although I was still totally secretive at work. It turned out that work was very interesting, but I was getting so little money that I had no money to eat. The salary structure TBL had was set up for three or four people to share an apartment and car. But I was alone. I did many telexes to TBL to no avail. They didn't respond to my requests.

I finally quit that job and decided to move to Washington, DC. Right after I quit the job, TBL increased my salary by three times. But it was too late for me to go back.

Ed, my friend from Harrisburg had moved to Washington, DC. He found a job for me in DC at Burroughs and invited me to live with him.

A few months after I got to Washington, I passed a guy on the street near my apartment. We both looked back at each other and I realized I had seen him before. Suddenly, I remembered that we had played together at a bathhouse the week before.

I greeted him, but he made a gesture indicating that he couldn't hear me. At the bathhouse, I hadn't realized he was deaf. It's not uncommon for guys to have sex without speaking at the bathhouses. So, we wrote notes to each other, introduced ourselves, and decided to meet the next day at a restaurant.

At the restaurant, Justin handed me a sign language card that showed the signs of different letters. I looked at the card and gave it back to him. Justin shrugged as if he thought I was not interested. But I started to sign words as I spoke to him, though not perfect. Justin was really surprised and he asked me if I knew sign language before. I signed no. That was the beginning of my learning sign language.

Justin was deaf *and* mute. We became instant friends especially since I picked up sign language very fast. We started spending all our evenings together and we became lovers. It's interesting. When I first met him, his name was Marvin Evink. But after his biological father died (whom he was named after), he changed his name to Justin Evink because his father's obituary didn't have any mention of him and he really never knew him.

It's fascinating how you were able to pick up sign language almost instantly.

I have a sort of photographic memory. It shows up in interesting ways. I was once dating a Black guy who worked at The Pentagon as an illustrator. His name is Chuck Johnson. On our second date, he came to my house and brought small slides of his paintings. I looked at them and immediately recognized them. Years earlier, I had seen them in an inflight magazine. One was a painting of a woman hanging her laundry on a line and one was of a motorcycle. They were very realistic. I mentioned this to him and he was flabbergasted. He said they were indeed published in the magazine and he just couldn't understand how I could remember them from years before. Today, Chuck's a big-time artist. He lives in Memphis and he is still my friend.

That is amazing. Now, when you started dating Justin, were you still living with Ed?

Oh yes. Ed and I had a strange relationship. I was in love with him, but he liked me as a friend, not as a lover. I slowly understood that and fell out of love and into a friendship, which lasted until his death in 2009. Ed became a father figure for me, in my US family.

At that time, I bought my first apartment at River Place in Arlington, Virginia, and over the next few months, Justin and I developed our relationship. I got to know his friends, most of whom were also deaf.

Six months into the relationship, my sign language became so good that Justin's friends didn't believe that I was not deaf. Usually, when hearing people use sign language, it is different than when deaf people use it. Deaf people can tell the difference.

It reminded me of a story from *Mahabharat*. Raja Dhritarashtra married Gandhari. When she found out that her would-be husband was born blind, she decided to blindfold herself in order to be like her husband. Like Gandhari, I too decided to be deaf.

Once, we were at Gallaudet College (the university for the deaf), and some deaf people had a bet. To show that I could hear, one of the guys came behind me and yelled. I honestly didn't hear him (I actually remember hearing him, but in a strange way, it did not alarm me when he yelled).

You told me that before you came to the US, you weren't particularly interested in leaving India. What changed your mind? Was it because of the freedom you found in living openly as a gay man?

Well, I really wasn't out and open for a long time. It was several years before I acknowledged being gay to anyone at work. Being gay was part of why I stayed, but Indian immigration to the US is interesting. When I came here in 1979, I met many Indians who had settled down here. All their friends were Indians. They hardly had any American social contacts besides the ones they worked with. They had formed a "Little India" community here and dreamt of one day returning home.

Whenever they got together, they only talked about India. Yet, none of them ever moved back to India. Initially, their excuse used to be "a better job opportunity." Later it was "for the kid's education." After the kids were grown up, it was "for the grandkids."

In my case, I decided to stay here because I fell in love with a man. And, yes, leading a gay life here was much easier than in India. But I wrestled over the decision to stay here. My love of Indian culture, music, family and friends, and national pride was holding me back from deciding to stay and settle down here.

I could have rationalized my decision to stay here, as so many Indians do, by promising myself that one day I will return to India. But I told myself that if I stay here, I will have to become part of this society and not plan on someday returning home. The other option was to just return to India and lead a happy life there. So, yes, one of the things that pushed me to stay in the US was the fact that I was gay. I chose to stay and have never regretted it.

Four

I recorded our session last week and I transcribed our conversation. I'm sure I didn't get it all perfectly, but take a look and tell me what you think.

Wow. It looks great. I didn't think my speech was understandable enough for you to transcribe it.

What do you mean?

In my mind when I am speaking, I have some word that I want to say but I cannot find it. So, I substitute with another word and hope that the meaning come across.

I think you speak better than you think you do. Now, last week, I asked you to take note of your thoughts and emotions. How did that go?

I did it for three days and it didn't seem to help me. I didn't know what to write most of the time. What did you call it?

Cognitive-behavioral strategy. But, it's okay. There are many different techniques for dealing with our thoughts and emotions

and this is one of them. As I mentioned when we first met, I focus mainly on developing a relationship with my clients and that becomes the foundation of healing and growth. So don't worry about that exercise.

Good. I didn't find it helpful.

Last week, you were telling me that you struggled with your decision to stay in the US. I was wondering, was it mostly about leaving your family?

That was part of it, of course. I was very close to my family, especially my mother. But also, many parts of my culture. I think I told you earlier that I briefly considered a career in music. And, there are other aspects of culture such as food and language that all have a sort of pull. But ultimately, as I told you, I fell in love with a man and that became the thing that made me stay in the USA.

I thought of my decision a lot. As I told you before, I saw the other Indians who stayed here for the money and said they will go back someday, but never did. So, when I decided to "stay," it was going to be "stay for good." I was going to live like an "American," not like an "Indian in America." And while I've never regretted my decision or looked back, I appreciate all that I left behind, especially family.

Your family is in Mumbai?

Yes. I was born in Dahanu, a town about one hundred miles north of Bombay. That was in June 1955 and my parents lived in Bombay at the time. My mother went to my uncle's place in Dahanu for delivery. My mother and I came back to Bombay when she was well enough to do housework.

My father visited us on weekends while we were in Dahanu. In the Indian tradition, I was not given a name until I was twenty-one-days-old, at which time a naming ceremony was held there.

My father, being a very imaginative man, announced a contest to suggest a suitable name for me. The idea of a contest for picking a child's name was novel and daring at the time. The winner of the contest was to receive a box of sweets.

Out of the suggestions received, my parents ended up selecting the one that was nominated by my mother: Vishwas. In Marathi, it means "trust" or "belief." The other name my mother had suggested was Vikram. Vikram means "victor." Years later when I was in America and was looking for a suitable nickname for me that would be easier for my American friends to pronounce, I selected "Victor." It was my mother's second choice for my name, it started with V as Vishwas, so I didn't feel it was too alien to me.

Do you have fond memories of your childhood?

My early childhood memories are not as much "my" memories as they are recollections of stories my father told about my childhood.

Today, I am not sure if I remember the actual images from the incidents or just the stories that my father used to tell.

We lived in Khotachi Waadi in a single-room apartment in a run-down chawl. Khotachi Waadi used to be the most densely populated part of Bombay (now Mumbai). Among the buildings, most are chawls abutting each other. We lived in a ten-foot by ten-foot room that was divided into a small washing area, a small cooking area, and a bed. There was a small balcony outside that overlooked the backside of another chawl and offered a view of garbage thrown by people in the next building. Many of the stairs leading up to our room were broken and we had to walk very carefully to avoid falling in.

Despite what now may seem like a dire environment, my memories of growing up at the time are quite pleasant. A child does not need plush surroundings to be happy. My happiness came from holding the end of my mother's sari when she took me to a day-care center so that she could go to a sewing class, seeing my mother come back from the class to pick me up, waking up from an afternoon nap, finding a glucose biscuit (a cookie) sitting beside the bed for me, seeing my father come home at the end of the day, playing with other kids in the chawl, and all the love I received from my parents and neighbors.

When I was five years old, we moved to a place that had two rooms and a balcony. We shared the bathroom with one other family. But it was in a nicer area. This is where I spent all my school years.

My father was a civil engineer working for the Bombay Municipal Corporation. When they were building new roads or sewer lines, sometimes he used to work the night shift to supervise the construction or pouring of asphalt. He used to take me to work from time to time.

So, you must have inherited some of your intelligence and aptitude for engineering from your father.

I don't know about intelligence or aptitude. But, I realized that something was different about me when I was in college at Benaras.

That reminds me of something. In my second year of college, I went to my mother's childhood place, and there I met her aunt. She was so proud of me for going to the best school in India. She said, "That school was made for bright students like you. Only brahmins would be allowed."

I said, "Yes, all my friends are brahmins." She asked me their last names. I told her, "Abhyankar, Hirve, More, Bagde, and others." She said only "Abhyankar" seems like a brahmin—the others are not.

My parents never talked about caste. I didn't grow up with the concept that I am a brahmin and others are of various castes. Nevertheless, caste is a very big concept in India. Later at BHU, I learned about people's castes via my friend Bindu.

Your parents were not traditional in their thinking about caste. So, they didn't try to arrange a marriage for you?

No, they didn't. But that reminds me of a story. Guruji (my music teacher) had two sons and a niece. They all lived together. He used to take me and Urvi, a girl in my class, to his home after the class. There would always be something special such as pohe, sheera, or samosa, always cooked by his niece. Sometimes, he used to invite me alone to eat these yummy items. He would always emphasize to me that his niece made these.

When I was coming to the USA, he asked me about my marriage plans. I said it's too early to think about these things. Urvi later told me the plan was to get me married to the niece. And, I cannot remember what she looked like or even knowing her. But she was always around so I must have known her. Apparently, she cried when I left for the USA, and later when she was getting married, she confided in Urvi, "My husband is good, but not as good as Vishwas." When Urvi told me this, I was totally flabbergasted.

And were your parents receptive when you did come out to them?

They still had very traditional ideas about family and marriage. Before I had my first lover (Jimmy), I really didn't understand being gay. I just knew I wasn't attracted to women the way other guys were.

In college, I read a book by Bertrand Russell called *Marriage and Morals*. He described that in the future, both men and women will be working, and their children will be raised by institutions. I liked that theory. I professed it to my mother as a way to say I am not going to get married.

And I told you that I tried to introduce her to my first lover, Jimmy, and when she said she didn't have a good feeling about him, I just dropped the subject.

Vishwas, 1974

My mother, me, and my brother Avinash; my grandmother, brother Sudhanvshu, and my father, 1984

But you came out to her on some level that time when you met your friend in New York. And I'm assuming you talked to her about it later after you had lived in the USA, right?

It was much later. Coming to the USA just opened a whole smorgasbord of gay life to me. And when I returned to India, I thought that that was the end of it. I thought that I was not going to come back to the States. And the first thing I wanted to do was tell my close friends that I'm gay.

In my five years of college, I developed a close bond with three other guys. Kale was bright, Hirve was free-spirited, and Amrut was good-looking. For a while, I considered them as three individual friends. Then one evening, we four went to the Ganges River. There were four planks to get onto the pontoon bridge. Jokingly, Amrut said, "*Shevati aapan choughach*" ("After all, we are a foursome"). That incident made our foursome fixed.

When I came back after my first year in Pennsylvania, I was eager to come out to these close friends. I got quite different reactions from each of them.

Kale was very bright, a little awkward, and understood the basis of class problems, exactly like I used to. I remember the time we were going to the exam, and I had not studied for it, Kale told me the formulas. I aced the exam simply knowing the formulas. That is how I learned in college. I used to sit in a class and get the point or the basis of the class and I could extrapolate all the rest. I never studied but I aced all the exams.

Kale's response when I came out to him was, "Yep. I know." That was it.

In 1982, Kale also came to SUNY and finished his PhD. He has been my very dear and longest friend in the US. He is now a senior professor at the University of Illinois at Urbana-Champaign.

Amrut also had very little reaction. He was just kinda like, "Okay, whatever." These first two, Kale and Amrut, were basically saying, "We still love you," and they didn't have any objection to it at all.

Hirve had an interesting reaction. We met in a Chinese restaurant and when I told him, he said, "Oh, I thought you were bi," and he went on to express that being bi is the ideal thing because you can have sex with anyone. "You're just gay and I'm straight," he said, "so, we missed out on one of us being bi." I thought that was a very interesting reaction.

Oh, and one other friend of mine was dating his first cousin (which is frowned upon, because of social stigma and especially because their children can develop deformities), and when I came out to him, he sort of got excited. He said, "When I marry her, you can be the sperm donor so we can have a healthy child." That never happened, of course! Ha-ha.

Even though my friends didn't show any concern or resistance to my being gay, I still didn't come out to my mom at that time. When I came to India after being in Australia, I decided I have to tell my mother. But, I was there just for a week to get my visa renewed for going back to the USA, so I didn't have the conversation at that time either.

Two years after I moved to Washington, DC, and after I had been living with Justin, I went to India and I finally told her that I'm gay. But she didn't understand the concept of gay. It was never talked about in India. It's not like Christianity, or Islam, or Judaism, where they condemned the practice of being gay. It just was not talked about. It was not on anyone's radar that this is possible. So, my mother didn't understand what it was.

Are your parents still with us?

My mother died of lung cancer in 1985. She had lung cancer, though she never smoked. I went to India when she was in the hospital having chemotherapy. I got to spend some time with her. But soon after I got back, she passed away. For the first two months, I was numb. Like she was still alive. Then one day, I woke up and felt that she was gone. I burst out crying.

My father came to the US soon after she died with my brother Sudhanvshu. Two years later, I brought Sudhanvshu over here. My father came here twice after that. But in 1995, he also passed away in India. My brother Avinash took care of him at the end.

Did you ever come out to your father?

I never really had an open conversation with my dad about being gay. But I never hid it from him. He knew I was always with men. He visited me when Justin and I were sleeping in the same bed. And one time, he called me from my uncle's house. He said, "Your uncle is asking me why you are not getting married. Should I tell him that?" (He didn't specify what "that" meant.)

I replied, "Sure," and he said, "Your uncle is telling me not to say anything. He doesn't want to know." My father and I never had an open conversation about my being gay.

My mom was very open and accepting, but she expressed her concern that when I'm old, there should be someone to take care of me. I told her, "My friend Justin will be there for me."

That satisfied her, and from then onward, my parents wrote to Justin every time they wrote a letter to me. When they sent me a gift, they sent him the same gift. They treated him in every way as if he was my spouse.

Five

Good afternoon, Vishwas. How are you feeling this week? You don't seem like your normal sparkling self.

I'm not feeling so well actually.

Physically?

Yes, everything is more difficult since my stroke. My body and my brain don't work like they used to. I did some reading about psychology and suicide and I have come to the conclusion that the profession is misguided in its stance.

So, you have been thinking about suicide more this week?

As I told you before, I'm not depressed or unhappy (in spite of how difficult things sometimes get). I just don't want to get to a place where I lose all control and I get trapped in the medical system with no way out.

I understand your frustration and my profession's view of suicide may be misguided as you say. I'm curious about how things have changed since your stroke compared to how you

dealt with these same concerns for all those years dealing with the uncertainty of AIDS. I wonder if you would tell me about becoming HIV-positive and how you dealt with that for—what has it been—thirty years?

It's been thirty years since I tested positive, but I probably had HIV for a few years before the test was available.

We were hearing of a "gay plague" going around but didn't know what caused it and how it affected only gay people. Later, it was discovered to be caused by a virus, but there was no diagnostic test at the time. It took two more years to develop HIV tests.

Did you have friends with AIDS in those early days?

Yes, I knew several people who got AIDS back then. In 1983, I had a very good friend, David Blinkenstaff, who was the chef at Fireplace, a restaurant near Dupont Circle. Once, I had him over for dinner and made tandoori chicken, cumin rice, and cucumber raita. He liked it so much that he turned it into a special dish at his restaurant and called it "Chicken Vishwas." I went there for dinner one night with another friend of mine. The waiter explained that the dish was the chef's creation inspired by French cuisine. We got a kick out of it.

Then, David suddenly vanished. He did not show up at work and none of his friends knew where he was. He would not answer my calls. Then, I ran into his nephew whom I had met once with David. After pressing him hard for a while, he told me that David was at his parents' place in Hagerstown. It turns out that he had AIDS. He was quite sick and living with his parents.

I found his phone number from directory assistance and talked to him. He initially asked me not to come to visit, but I insisted, so he gave me his address. I drove up to Hagerstown one weekend. When he opened the door, I hugged him and he started to cry. He said no one had touched him since he got sick.

A couple of months later, he passed away. Once again, I ran into David's nephew on the street. He told me that, after David died, there was a story in the local newspaper in Hagerstown that mentioned that he had AIDS. After the story came out, people stopped going to the local bakery owned by David's parents. Eventually, they had to shut down the business.

It was a shameful time in our history. Fear brings out the worst in people.

In 1986, when the first HIV test was available, the insurance companies started dropping people who were positive. People were dying and society was turning its back on them.

I waited for an anonymous test to become available. Finally, it was offered in Maryland. My friends, Chuck and Sig, let me use their zip code and I got the test. As I suspected, the result was positive. The doctor said I had one to two years to live. I'm sure I had been positive for years before they knew what it was or how it was transmitted.

Justin and I had been together since 1981 and it had been three years since I bought the condo at River Place. At that time, I was looking to buy a house. But when I found out I had only a year or so to live, I told my realtor to stop looking for houses.

My agent (who was also gay) suggested that I go ahead and buy the house and get a policy that would pay off the mortgage if I died. That way, I could make Justin my successor so he would get the house when I died. I bought the house and Justin and I moved in together.

That was a very loving thing for you to do for Justin.

I had a very special bond with Justin. Because of my skill at picking up sign language, I became his mouthpiece in some ways. Learning the language so quickly and completely wasn't surprising to me. I have a photographic memory. But, I also learned that my brain could partition in surprising ways. There were a few Marathi-speaking friends at Gallaudet (the university for the deaf) and they were fascinated that I could speak to them in Marathi, but simultaneously sign in English.

But Justin opened up my world as well. I became part of the deaf community and Justin was well-connected in the gay community as well. We didn't have much money in the beginning and Justin took me camping. We couldn't afford to stay in a hotel at the beach, so we would drive to Rehoboth and camp just outside of town. Then we could still go to the beach and enjoy the gay parties.

I remember Justin would sit backward in the passenger seat while I was driving. That way, he could sign and we could carry on a conversation while I was driving.

We had a lot of fun. And, it was also a very sad time because of AIDS. Over the next several years, most of our friends died one by one.

I can't imagine how horrible that must have been. And, it must have been so hard on your relationship with Justin as well.

Justin and I had an open relationship. Well, in the beginning, we were just friends and did things together. Then slowly, it grew into a love relationship. But it was always an open relationship. While we were together, Justin had ongoing relationships with three other men. The third of these men was a very interesting guy named Ron. He had been the architect of The White House for sixteen years. He gave us private tours of The White House and invited us to some interesting events.

Justin was into flowers and gardening and Ron was also into that. Ron helped to design our backyard and patio. They did a lot of work in our yard. They were proud of all the things they had done.

Justin's relationship with Ron went on for many years. Then in 1991, I met Joe.

Justin always wanted an open relationship with me, but when I met Joe, Justin didn't take it well. He met Joe when I first started seeing him, but when he realized that Joe was now a part of my life, he stopped speaking to him. He told me he was uncomfortable. Then, after I had known Joe for a year, he started speaking with him and he was okay with him and considered him a friend.

You were with Justin for about ten years then by the time you met Joe in 1991?

Yes. Justin and I met in 1981. I met Joe in 1991.

In the late eighties when the test became available in Virginia, Justin took it, and he was also positive. We had assumed he would be too when I learned that I was positive.

Years later, Ron had AIDS and he moved to San Francisco, where he later died. Justin didn't take it well. He did a lot of introspection and decided to try living alone, a fantasy he had for a long time. We both knew we had a short time to live. Justin realized that since he became aware of his sexuality, he always had been living with someone else. He wanted to try to live on his own.

He said he wanted to party and enjoy the time he had left. I told him it wasn't a good idea, because of his health. But, this is what he wanted, and so, he found an apartment in DC and moved in by himself.

Justin moved into his own place in 1992 and he died in 1995. He ended his life the way he wanted to live.

That way of living was not my idea. My idea was to survive.

Vishwas & Justin, 1982   *Justin, 1993*

And amazingly, you did survive. I'm sure it wasn't easy.

I just kept doing the next thing and as in the "Gay Crow" story I told you, I just kept looking for the positive. I know it's not common, but I kept a fairly positive attitude most of the time. Even at the beginning. What could I do? I just kept going forward.

After I took my first HIV test, I came home knowing that I had to wait for a week to get the results. When I called for the results of the HIV test, they told me I had to go and meet with a lady at their office. She told me that I was positive and gave me some documents. I told her that I had to die someday and that I was okay. This way I know that I had a year or so, I was fine with that. She urged me to find a doctor.

Driving home, I was kind of numb. I thought of all the men I had sex with. I could not figure out which one (or ones) gave me the infection. Then again, I thought, *I am going to die anyway. Why should I care about when?*

Vishwas, you are hyper-logical.

What does that mean?

Your thinking is totally logical, but most people let their emotions get in the way and don't go that far in logic.

I think you are right. By the time I got home, it was settled in my mind. I was at peace with what the doctors were saying about how long I had to live. But I kept my attention on good things like the promotion I received at work that same week.

Yet, I had some emotional moments as well. I had set up a date with Chuck for that evening. Suddenly, it hit me that I could not have sex anymore and fear came over me. I could not imagine living with no sex until I died.

I was still in that state when the doorbell rang. I opened the door and Chuck was standing there. He reached to hug me. I pulled back and said, "I had the test and I am HIV-positive." He didn't blink. He said, "We have always had safe sex. This doesn't change anything. We can still have safe sex." Hearing that put my mind at ease. This was the only time I had a panic attack about this and it lasted for maybe two hours.

That's still quite impressive to process through something so quickly. And after you got your results, there weren't many clinics treating HIV at the beginning, were there?

That's right. This happened in July 1986. Through my friends, I found Dr. Caceras, an older doctor with a two-level clinic in a Q Street townhouse. The person at the front desk would enter the information into a Tandy computer and hand me a floppy disk. (In those days, having a computer in the office was a novelty.) Then I saw the PA for vitals and blood tests. He put those results on the record and then I took the disk to the doctor. He inserted it into his computer to enter the diagnosis. I told him my diagnosis. He ordered another blood test (ELISA) to confirm the diagnosis.

Two weeks after the ELISA test, the results confirmed that I had HIV. There was no treatment for it. Dr. Caceras told me that I had one year to live.

More than a year later, in December 1987, AZT became available. This was the first approved HIV medicine. When the doctor prescribed it to me, I decided to start taking it the next day. I took it in the morning on the way to a meeting in Pennsylvania. It was a mistake. I threw up on the way. AZT wasn't suitable for my constitution. I checked with my doctor. He said to take the pills less often; some would be better than none.

I took the AZT for around three years. It didn't seem to do anything. So, in November 1990, I stopped it. There was no other drug available until April 1992. Then DDI became available. It was a tablet that you dissolve in water like Alka-Seltzer and drink thirty minutes before eating.

By April 1994, I developed unbearable peripheral neuropathy as a side effect and had to stop DDI. In January 1995, I started on d4T (that was later called Zerit) and in November 1995, I stopped d4T and started taking Saquinavir, a protease inhibitor.

By the end of 1995, I had developed resistance to all the existing meds. I had lost a lot of weight, had no appetite, and no energy. My T-cells were 185. That's below the threshold of 200 set by the FDA for the AIDS diagnosis. Now, I was not just HIV-positive—I had AIDS. This meant I was eligible for permanent disability. The doctor said I should stop working and enjoy the few months to a year I had left.

After working eighteen years, I had saved only $100K (which we owed on the house). But I had done something smart early on: I had a long-term disability insurance policy that paid 60 percent of my salary till I die or become eligible for SSA.

So, that's when you went on disability and stopped working?

Yes. A year later, it was discovered that protease inhibitors are never to be taken by themselves. The virus developed resistance to it right away. But it was too late for me. By April 1996, I started taking a three-drug combination of Ritonavir (Norvir), AZT, and 3TC. Ritonavir is a weak protease inhibitor, but it was the only one available at that time.

Listening to all that you've endured, I'm amazed that you are alive to tell the story.

Well, in a way, I'm one of the lucky ones. So many died along the way, and not just from HIV and AIDS.

My friend Ken Hockenberry is a good example. He was from Kentucky. He always told us about his classmate Mitchell McConnell (the Kentucky senator). He said he was the same back in high school, an asshole from that time until now. Ken also told us about a time when his older brother brought a Black friend to their house. He went by the name of Cassius Clay.

Muhammed Ali?

Yes. And, Ken's father scolded him for bringing him to the home and told him never to socialize with him again. Anyway, Ken was a dear friend, and Justin and I went to Ken's place for the Kentucky Derby a couple of times. He died later in about 99 or 2000. He had moved to Mexico—Ken was fond of young, Hispanic men. He was taking some blood pressure medicine that was approved at that time. Later, we learned that the safety testing had not been done properly and lots of people died from that medicine. Now it's illegal, but it was approved inappropriately at the time.

Well, you are one of the lucky ones indeed. You've survived in the face of incredible odds, but you've also had an amazing life.

I *have* an amazing life.

It's good to hear you say that.

Six

You were telling me last week about your experience with HIV/ AIDS. I was struck by how you seemed to make your peace with dying very early when you were diagnosed.

I did. I didn't see any point in complaining or feeling sorry for myself. I just kept looking at the next thing there was to do and asking, *How can I make the most of the time I have left?*

I know you endured a great deal of pain and suffering along with the uncertainty during those decades. Did you ever contemplate suicide back then?

Oh, that reminds me. I found a note that I wrote back in 1999. I wrote it one night when I couldn't sleep. It addresses your question. The answer to your question is that I didn't consider suicide. I thought I was about to die several times, but I never wished for death.

Oh, you brought the letter in? Please, read it to me.

Sunday, September 12, 1999

It's 1:26 a.m. and I can't sleep.

I hate to use superlatives like "lowest"... it's so American though; they (and now I too) like to describe everything in extremes. Statements like "I love marmalade" and "I hate rain" make the range between love and hate so narrow that all attributes now have to crowd over one end or the other. Clearly on a linear scale, "I love Joe" is a far ways left of "I love Pepsi" and "I hate rapists" is a far ways right of "I hate rain." Yesterday, or should I say today, since I haven't gone to bed yet, must have been one of the lowest points in my battling this illness.

Just as the first sentence of this note doesn't mean hatred at all. It simply means I would rather describe feelings more accurately with a wide range of words and try to fit my life into two categories: love and hate. People talk about "the worst driver ever," "the best thing since sliced bread" and "sexiest man in America" when it will take ten seconds to come up with a million examples that would disprove the statements. I used to get such a kick out of this "extremism" in America that I had toyed about an award for the "most moderate person," which of course I would have won.

Moderation is my motto. It was instilled in me by my mother, along with the quest to find the center ("*Sthitaprajna ho*," she used to say), always seek and expose the truth.

Days like this make me turn my attention inside and re-consider the value of life, quality of life, and the trade-offs therein. Such days are becoming more frequent lately. Maybe it has something to do with the end of the summer and the fall. Last year, I went through a similar crisis when I asked Dr. Rashbaum to stop all medication except the prophylaxes. We decided to take a drug holi-day to recover some quality of life. A year ago, about the same time, I was mired with anemia, constant fatigue, diarrhea, gases, bloating, nausea, and what have you.

When I look further back, it seems to be an annual pat-tern I have developed. The combination therapy I am taking seems to stop being effective around the same time of the year and the side effects become worse than the treatment itself. I have taken all HIV drugs that have been out on the market and find myself having to wait for some new drug to become available in a clinical trial or expanded access. Every new combination I try reduc-es the viral load and improves the T-cell count for a cou-ple of months and then stops being effective. Then we go through the same dilemma each year.

Is it better to stop all anti-HIV drugs and wait for a new drug to arrive on the market or is it better to stay on some treatment rather than none? Are the side effects making the quality of life so unbearable that the preven-tive drugs are not worth taking either?

Cycles in nature are common. Trees go through the cycle of shedding the leaves and sprouting new ones every year. Bears go into hibernation every winter. So maybe my body is simply going through its natural cyclical rhythm?

The current drug regimen gives me so many gastrointestinal problems that my mind keeps wondering about whether it is time to give in to the disease rather than keep fighting it. These are not suicidal thoughts. They are merely trying to assess the reality of the situation. To affect an attitude adjustment, if you may.

But there is no point mulling over the same things when I am trying to fall asleep.

That was 1999? You mentioned it as one of the lowest points in battling your illness.

I know I wrote that, but looking back on things, I don't remember things that way. At that moment, it may have felt like a low point, but somehow I don't remember most of the "bad" times as such. I remember the people and the projects and interesting things.

I suppose if I were to categorize the "bad times," it would include the several times I've been at death's door, so to speak, like when I got lymphoma. Those are probably some of the low points.

I get that. The letter reflects your Gay Crow way of looking at things. And you maintained that even those times when you were facing death. It's quite remarkable how resilient you were.

I was always just looking for the next thing to do and how to make the most of it at the time. I think I told you before about when I was diagnosed with AIDS in 1995 after Justin died. I went in for testing and that's when my T-cell count fell below two hundred, which is the threshold for AIDS. That's when my doctor recommended that I go on disability and enjoy what time I had left. So, I stopped working.

Joe had recently taken a new assignment down in Abilene, Texas. I would regularly travel to be with Joe down in Texas, and now that I was on disability, I thought I would just move to be with Joe wherever his career took him.

At that time, I had lost a lot of weight, I felt very weak, and I had no appetite. It felt like something could go wrong at any time. I called doctors and hospitals in the area and I couldn't find any doctor near Abilene who would take me on as a patient.

That was when the medical profession still didn't know what to do with AIDS and HIV patients. Many doctors tried to ignore it or just weren't very helpful.

Finally, I discovered one place in Abilene that took HIV patients. This clinic had one nurse and two rooms. The nurse was in the clinic for a few hours in the afternoons and she told me that the doctor comes in from Dallas to see patients once a month for four hours.

I kept calling around to find another doctor, but eventually, I came back to this clinic. The nurse said something like, "I knew you wouldn't find any other provider in this area." She set me up with a monthly appointment with the doctor. I asked her what I would do in an emergency.

"Don't have one," was her answer. That's when I knew this was not going to work for me.

I can't imagine what that must have been like for you. The medical system really failed in those early days of HIV/AIDS.

This was in 1995. HIV had been around and known since 1981. At the time I thought, *How can this be? There are three medical colleges in the immediate area, but all the doctors keep making excuses about not having the training or facilities to treat HIV patients.*

HIV was a gay disease to them. Since the rest of the population wasn't at risk, HIV treatment didn't get the attention and funding needed. What did you do?

I decided to keep getting my treatment in the DC area. I had not yet sold my house back in Virginia. For a while, I was spending two weeks with Joe in Abilene and then two weeks in Virginia. **That must have been very difficult given your condition.**

It was challenging. Eventually, Joe decided to quit his job and move back to Virginia with me. He was quite sure I had little time left, and he gave up his pension and benefits to be with me for whatever time was left. I still wasn't thinking that I was going to die soon, but Joe was more concerned about this.

I want to ask you more about Joe and your life together, but you were telling me about several times that you were, as you said, "at death's doorstep." This period when your T-cell count was below two hundred and you had trouble finding care was one of those times, right?

Yes. At the time, I didn't have any of the known AIDS symptoms until I was diagnosed with Stage IV non-Hodgkin's lymphoma in 2001. That was the first major AIDS-defining symptom I got. And that was when I said to myself, "Now this is the end of it." And the process of the treatment was really difficult because I had one week for the infusion there and then three weeks recovering. That first week went very, very bad, physically. But even then, mentally I was not thinking about it. My gay crow was still alive at that time.

It had to have been difficult to maintain a good outlook when everything in the medical field at that time looked quite hopeless for AIDS patients.

That's true. After I was treated for lymphoma, I broke my ankle and my doctor didn't want me to have the surgery to be able to walk again. He reasoned I was going to die soon and it wouldn't be worth the trouble.

Ugh!

I had already had all six treatments for lymphoma. It was an experimental treatment called "Epoch with R." The side effects were horrific. Today, they do three treatments for this, but then they gave six treatments. It also involved twelve rounds of spinal taps. I was so weak, I couldn't walk. I was just laying around and not doing anything.

It was Christmas Eve and Joe was preparing dinner. We were talking about our plans to go the next day to Pittsburgh to have Christmas dinner with Joe's family.

Joe put dinner on the table and I got up to walk to the dining room. As I approached the table, my legs collapsed under me and I fell to the floor. Joe rushed over to me and said that my leg was turned in an unnatural position.

I thought it was just a sprain, but the pain got increasingly intense and we decided to go to the emergency room. There we learned that I had broken my fibula and tibia just above the ankle. They wrapped it up, and since it was Christmas Eve, they couldn't do the surgery right away. They told us to call on Monday and schedule an appointment with an orthopedic surgeon.

The next morning, Joe and I were sitting around and I said to Joe, "Why don't we just go to Pittsburgh? I'm going to sit around here anyway. I might as well go and sit around there and we will be with your family."

The only problem was that we didn't have a wheelchair. So, when we got there, someone found a luggage cart. They lifted me onto the luggage cart and four people walked me up the stairs to the apartment.

The Gay Crow in action!

Precisely! And we had a great time.

And you're walking, so you must have gotten the surgery?

We saw the surgeon that week to schedule the surgery. The surgeon took Joe aside and asked if he should operate on the leg or just leave it as it was since it looked like I wasn't going to live long. I didn't want to live in a wheelchair, so we went ahead and scheduled the surgery.

And the surgery went well. They put eight screws and a plate to secure the ankle. The recovery took six months. I got a trainer from Pakistan at the gym, called Waqar. I restarted doing yoga and lifting weights. I was fit as ever.

And you recovered from the lymphoma?

Yes. The chemotherapy had done its job, but it left my T-cells very, very low, close to zero. That meant I had no resistance power to any infection. I started taking Diflucan twice a day to fight any infections that arose. It's usually taken for seven days, but I took it every day for four years until my viral load went down.

But, the next few years were a period of ups and downs with new medications and side effects. I would be on a medication for a period of time and the HIV would develop a resistance to it. Then the doctors would put me on another. Often, I was on multiple medications at once. They all have various side effects and none of them maintained effectiveness for very long.

In 2004, a friend of mine told me that the National Institutes of Health (NIH) was looking for cases for an HIV trial program. I applied and I was invited to participate in NIH trials. They took over all of my medical care during that time.

I'm noticing a pattern. When you were dealing with AIDS you were still the Gay Crow. You took charge, looked for the silver lining. When you talk about life since the stroke, it's really about a loss of control, and to some extent, a loss of this Gay Crow way of being.

You might be onto something there. I'll have to think about that.

I think there's more to it as well. You asked me to help you find a new "zest for life." I think it's not gone. Your zest is there, but it's buried somehow.

Let's keep looking for it then.

Seven

Last week, you were just starting to tell me about getting HIV treatment at NIH.

In 2004, my friend Steve (from Patrick and Steve) asked me if I wanted to go to NIH (National Institutes of Health). NIH is the nation's premier lab. They wanted a ton of documentation about my current condition. Fortunately, I had copies of all my records with me.

I met with someone at NIH. They interviewed me and gave me several blood tests (many tubes worth). Two weeks later, I got an email that I had been approved. That gave rise to a whole bunch of tests and treatments. Now, NIH was not just my primary care physician, but *all* my medical needs went through NIH. The main advantage of that was NIH covered all my prescription drugs, which had risen to roughly $6,000–$8,000 a month.

Another thing was that I was in a program at NIH called Infectious Disease Follow Up (IDFU), which meant any treatment they gave had to be approved, no experimental treatments were allowed.

Over the next four years, I had an oncologist, and I saw specialists for urinary, chest, stomach, endocrinology, walking, acupuncture, and had a swath of treatments done to me. Initially, I had to go to NIH three times a week. Later, it was once a week and then every two weeks. I got to know the staff very well.

Ever since my chemotherapy, my T-cell count was almost zero. It affected my overall health. By 2006, my virus had become resistant to all known drugs. I started having diarrhea. That's when I got the spot of Kaposi Sarcoma on my leg and there were many other symptoms as well.

Dr. Thomas Wright, who had scheduled a follow-up appointment for me in October, did not believe that I would make it. He assumed that I would be dead by then. Since there was no other FDA- approved therapy left for me to try, NIH could not treat me. But, they said that if I found some therapy or experimental drug that would help me, they would allow me to try it in addition to the NIH treatment.

This had to have been another one of the low points for you.

Really, the whole period from 2002 until 2006, my T-cells were zero and my viral load was up in the millions. I was always very vulnerable to infection, of course. But, this point with the NIH shook me up. This seemed to be the end of life for me.

My thoughts about this turned around quite rapidly though. At fifty-one years of life, the thought of dying didn't seem to be so bad. All I had to do was disconnect from everything on Earth.

I would soon be gone and my memories would fade from people's minds.

I slowly started to disassociate from people and feelings. Then, I disassociated with objects such as our house and cars. Then, I disassociated from my life expectations and desires. I prepared my mind clean, just like when I had decided to stay in the US and disassociate from life in India. I felt similar to the sannyasis, who let go of all the things they had as they prepared to die.

The one thing I could not disassociate from was Joe. I recognized that, for Joe, I would give life one more shot. If I succeed, well and good. If I don't, nothing is lost.

I sense a Gay Crow moment here.

I picked up the phone and called every pharmaceutical company I could find and asked them if they had any drugs in development that I could be part of. After five or ten calls, I got in touch with their lab team, test coordinator, or a lab doctor. They would say no and I would move on to the next phone number. Then, I began calling several labs, hospitals, research institutions, and doctors' offices to look for a new drug trial I could take part in. I must have made hundreds of such cold calls.

That's amazing, Vishwas.

Eventually, a coordinator in Houston gave me a number for someone in Philadelphia. I called them to discover that they were a test site, but their quota was full. I asked to put my name on their list, just in case one of their test subjects would drop out. Then the lady asked, "Have you checked with Georgetown Hospital? They are also testing this new drug, but they are also full." This was news to me. Georgetown was quite close to my home, but NIH didn't tell me about this. There was an NIH policy that they would not give another doctor's name or number.

I called Georgetown and talked to the coordinator there. She said their quota for the trial was also full. I requested my name to be added to the waiting list. She told me there was no chance that I would get anywhere. The list already had nine people on it. I insisted, however, and the lady took my name anyway.

Two weeks later, I received a call from Karen, a coordinator for Georgetown. One of the people in their study had dropped out. She had a chance to fill the slot. But, she had to fill it that day. She had called all nine people. For one reason or another, they were not available. I was the last person she called. They required a lot of testing and documentation. Fortunately, I had it all. One of the crucial tests was a resistance profile, which I had already done at NIH. When I had requested a copy, the nurse had said that they didn't give it out. But, I contacted the record-keeping department directly and they sent it to me.

With a stack of documentation, I hopped in the car with Joe and we went to their office. They were only thirty minutes from our home. We had every test they wanted. Karen was really surprised. Then a week later, I received the medicine made by Merck in a test bottle. I was very fortunate because, in this Phase III trial, there was a 60 percent chance that I received the actual drug and only a 40 percent chance that I would receive a placebo.

I had already coordinated with a doctor at NIH. We had decided to throw everything at the virus: Prezista, Norvir, Truvada, in addition to the new drug being tested. That included Fuzeon, which was the worst HIV drug. It involved mixing two vials into a drug that you inject twice-daily in your belly. It creates a beesting-like response and a node there.

That sounds horrible!

But I don't think of it that way. It was just another medicine to me.

Two weeks after starting the trial, I had a blood test. My viral load was down from 235,000 to 115. An astonishing feat! It had previously been up to over a million. I was definitely receiving the real drug and not the placebo. Two weeks later, I had another blood test. Lo and behold, my viral load was undetectable. This drug saved my life and the FDA approved it in two years. They named the new drug Isentress.

This changed everything for me. Over the course of six years, my T-cells went up to two hundred and now they are up to nine hundred, which took fourteen years. From this point in 2006, my viral load became what they call "undetectable," which also means I won't transmit the virus to others.

Since 2006, I call this my "life 2.0"

Vishwas, you have to find a way to share your story. It is truly inspiring.

I'd like to do that, but I don't know if people would understand me. I did get invited to share my story with a bunch of HIV researchers once.

Did you do it?

Yes. It was an unusual opportunity. Frank Maldarelli, an attending physician at NIH, also has an advanced research lab at Fort Detrick, Maryland. This is where some of the most advanced research by NIH is done.

I had always been curious to find out how they measure the virus, the T-cells, and other blood tests. I wanted to "see" the virus to know what I am fighting. I used to often ask Dr. Maldarelli if I could see this done in the lab. In December 2008, after the virus had become undetectable in my bloodstream, he invited me to take a tour of the labs in Fort Detrick. He mentioned that I would meet some people there who would like to ask me some questions before the tour and asked if it would be okay to disclose my name and background to them. This is almost never done because of the strict rules of patient confidentiality. I was more than happy to agree to this.

The day of the tour, something came up and Dr. Maldarelli could not go to Fort Detrick with us, but he arranged for a limo to take me and my partner, Joe, to the facility. I was expecting a small meeting on our arrival, followed by the tour. To my surprise, they ushered me into a big auditorium with over two hundred people attending. This was their monthly all-hands meeting and I was the sole "guest speaker" that day. I was totally unprepared for this. Maybe Dr. Maldarelli had planned to explain it to me on the drive to Fort Detrick.

How did it go?

The meeting started with a lady doctor who presented my case and medical history to the group with charts and graphs on the big screen. When I got on the podium, I said that I am totally unprepared for this and I have nothing to present, but I am willing to answer any questions on any topic without reservation.

Over the next hour or so, people asked me all sorts of questions like: "How did you get infected?", "How did you handle side effects of medications?", "How did your family, friends, and coworkers deal with it?", "What services will help people like you?", "To what do you attribute your survival?"

I really enjoyed sharing my story with them. No one had ever asked me all these questions and shown so much interest in my disease. People in the audience were doctors, researchers, scientists, lab technicians, and nurses.

After the talk, we went on a tour of the facility. We saw the machine where they extract the virus material from blood serum, the process that separates individual virus bodies and counts them, machines that measure T-cells. They explained how they do DNA analysis of the virus.

As I was going to different departments, people were coming up to me and thanking me for sharing my story with them. Some of them had never met an AIDS patient, let alone known him by his lab results and history.

One lady who runs the T-cell counter machine said, "Meeting you gave meaning to my work, which otherwise seems mechanical, routine, and boring." She explained that she comes in the morning, loads up the machine with some sealed tubes, and watches the computer screen all day as it spits out reports.

I told her, "While you are running this test, I am pacing up and down, waiting for the results with bated breath. So are each of the patients whose blood samples are going through your machine."

Months after that visit, I would still hear from NIH staff that people back in the labs still talk about me. I am still under the care of NIH.

Eight

Good afternoon, Vishwas. A couple sessions back, I mentioned a pattern I observed. I was comparing how you handled the challenge with AIDS for thirty years to how you have been dealing with your stroke.

Yes, I thought about what you said. It wasn't so much about the loss of my control over my condition. I had very little control over my HIV condition for most of the time since I got it.

But you *seized* control of the situation back then. You made all those calls and worked your way into trials that probably saved your life.

Yes, that's true. But I think the difference has had more to do with the diminishment of my abilities since the stroke. I lost half of my brain and I can't remember and I can't think quite like I used to be able to do.

And you felt you lost something of that Gay Crow spirit. Isn't that true?

Well, it certainly is more difficult to see the bright side some days.

Both of those qualities are essential features of your sense of yourself. You see yourself as a thinker, a problem solver, and as that guy who can focus on the good in spite of difficulties.

That's true.

But I think there's more to it than that. I think you live for a challenge.

Challenge in a particular sense perhaps. I've often thought that since childhood, I've been driven by curiosity. I want to know how things work. I like the challenge of making sense of a thing.

I can see how you brought that sense of curiosity to your AIDS journey. I imagine it shows up in other aspects of your life as well.

I'm sure it's been the prime driver of my career success.

Yes. That makes sense. I don't know much about your career except that you are an engineer and your first job brought you to America. Let's talk about your career.

Well, after I worked with Tata Burroughs for a few years (that's the company that hired me out of IIT in India), I went to work with Burroughs in the US. It's like two totally different companies. That was back in 1981. Ed helped me get that job in Washington, DC.

84

My first project was the logistics system at Walter Reed Medical Center. The project was to manage the inventory and supplies to the nursing station.

They had a big computer set up there. Computers used to be kept at a very low temperature. I was amused at the play with the heating systems. In winter, my car had a heater, I wore a parka when I got out of the car, then I went into the warm building. In the building, there was a cold room for the computer. Inside the cooled computer room, the operators had an office with heaters. In the heated office, there was a small refrigerator to keep their lunch cold.

So, it was cold inside of hot, inside of cold, and so on.

I found that amusing.

And what was challenging about your job?

At first, I had a real problem with my accent, which I thought would be hard to understand over the phone. But soon I realized that it wasn't bad. I got over that very quickly.

The work itself was usually challenging. Going between McLean, where my office was, and Walter Reed in DC. Meeting the clients (usually lieutenant colonels) and seeing the computers. It kept my curiosity engaged.

My next project at Walter Reed was to automate the food service. Everything from designing the menus, handling the diets, to recipes, to delivering the food to the patients.

I was sitting at my desk, concentrating on the food service project, when Lloyd Johnson walked in and said, "There's a new and exciting project coming up and I signed up for it. I think that you can do it." The project was with the Defense Intelligence Agency (DIA) in Battle Creek, Michigan, to design their transaction system.

A transaction system includes a controller, a language, and several modules. I made a few trips to Battle Creek, Michigan, to collect all the requirements from the users. And I designed the system. My final presentation was scheduled to be in January 1984. It gave me an idea.

I renamed the slides with Big Brother, Newspeak, Winston, Julia, and Ministry of Truth.

1984. George Orwell. That's funny! You made your own creative challenge there.

Yes. It was fun. But I didn't tell anyone about it. I was going to Michigan with Lloyd. I was excited about my *1984* references and I could not contain myself, so I told Lloyd that I had renamed all the modules to match with the *1984* characters. I thought he would be just as excited as me, but he was not amused. I told him,

"It is too late to change it now." We got into Battle Creek late in the evening. My presentation was the next morning at 8 a.m.

In his introduction, Lloyd apologized for the naming convention. Then I began my presentation. On the first slide, I mentioned Big Brother and I heard a chuckle in the audience. The next slide had the Newspeak as the language in which to define the process. The whole audience laughed. Then as the presentation went on, people in the audience got very involved and told me what additional modules would be called. The presentation became a big success. What could have been a tedious and routine system became very interesting and engaging.

They probably weren't expecting an engineer to be so creative and humorous. I'm curious. Were you out to your coworkers back then?

Generally not. In my programmers team, there was one guy called Bob Morrow. He was a tall, lean guy with an adorable smile. Bob and I used to get along well. Once we were chatting, and he asked me what I did over the weekend, and where I go. I told him that I was going downtown. But I didn't say where I would go. He told me that he goes to "The Bookstore," a bar on 22nd Street in Northwest DC. I knew that bar, but I had never gone in. In the neighborhood, there were three other gay bars. I used to go to them. But I didn't want to tell him. He said next weekend, he would drive, and we would go to The Bookstore.

So the next weekend, he was driving, and I was in the passenger seat. He said, "Instead of The Bookstore, let's go to the Lost and Found." It's another bar in Southeast DC, and they have good music and dancing. Lost and Found was a friendly gay bar. I used to like going there to dance. Some straight people went there too. So, we went there. After a drink and talking about work things, he said, "Do you want to dance?" I was anxious to dance.

When we were dancing, Bob asked me, "Is this your kind of place?" I said yes. He said, "I thought so." Then I realized that he is gay too. We had a friendly chat after that. It was understood that this secret was staying with us and not to be spoken of at work.

And you stayed closeted after you were diagnosed with HIV?

Definitely. HIV made many gay people go back into the closet because the general public became worried about AIDS. It became even more difficult to come out as I became more visible and advanced in the organization.

The same week I first got tested for HIV in 1986, I was selected to join a group called "HiPo." It's a group of High Potential individuals deemed suitable to become vice president and above in the company. There were several meetings of the group and each of us was matched up with a mentor. My mentor was a vice president from Sperry Corporation. We met with the mentor once a week and received advice.

Earlier that year, Burroughs and Sperry Corporation had merged and formed Unisys. A billion-dollar project came along (back when a billion dollars was a big deal). I was made the chief engineer for this project, called "Quest." It was a proposal of a system of software, hardware, and network computers to service all of the US military services. The winner of this contract would be a major provider for the US military.

This is the time I remember very well how I trained myself to think like ordinary people. As I told you, I had this photographic memory. I remembered every item in the Request for Proposal. Once something came up, and I began to chatter off the item and our response to it. The project manager said, "Woah, woah! You are too fast for me." That's when I realized that I should not be like that. I should speak like the regular people and slow down.

There was a team of one hundred people involved. It was a collaboration between Unisys and Intel. It took over two years of time and involved working on the proposal in Washington, DC, and later we conducted a benchmark in Phoenix, Arizona. I worked on the project for long hours and many weekends. Our proposal included thirty boxes of material. We didn't win the contract on price. We were first in terms of technical points, but not on cost. The company that won it had underbid.

That sounds very stressful. You're doing all of this while living with a death sentence due to your HIV.

It was stressful. This project went on for a year. I was going into the bathroom and taking pills throughout the day, always careful that no one found out.

But, see that's the thing. This was my life and this is where I focused my attention. I did what I needed to do with the HIV, but I never allowed myself to dwell on that. I had an exciting career. I had two great loves in my life, and wonderful friends.

You were determined not to let HIV define you or your life. I get it.

Precisely. And I wasn't ignoring my condition either. At one point, I charted the progress of my T-cell counts after all the projects I had worked on. It showed that after each of these projects, my T-cell count went down, never to be raised again. That is when I decided that I had to slow down this trend if I was to survive this disease. Nevertheless, I kept getting promoted.

I think your experience supports my theory that much of the "zest" of your life comes from creatively solving problems and overcoming challenges.

I think that's true. That and figuring out how things work.

Do you think that's what's missing in your life since your stroke? Do you think it could be as simple as finding some problem to solve or figuring out how something works?

Hmm. I've been thinking more along the lines that I don't have the faculties I used to, but you may be onto something there. I don't know what would hold the interest for me and stimulate my curiosity.

Vishwas, it's hard for me to believe you have lost your curiosity. It's one of your defining qualities. You are inherently curious and it's just who you *are*.

There is one thing that I've begun to think a lot about lately and it has stirred my curiosity.

What is that?

What you do. How psychology or therapy works.

That's very interesting. So, you think therapy is working for you?

Yes. I think it is helping me. It's not exactly what I expected therapy to be like, but for me, the relationship with you is what has made the difference.

I'm delighted to hear that. It's hard to know from week to week how things are actually going for you. Just out of curiosity, what did you expect or what's different than what you expected?

I don't know. I guess I had pictures in my head of lying down and telling you about my dreams.

That's more of a Freudian or Jungian analysis thing. But sometimes, dreams can be helpful in therapy. Especially when clients have recurring dreams or nightmares.

I've had a couple of those. I used to have the same nightmare about a truck quite often. I was always in the driver seat of a big sixteen-wheeler truck and I lost control of the truck. This was back when I worked for Burroughs.

One day, Lloyd told me that we had to go to Kentucky to get the functional requirements for a contract with Ford Motor Company. The plant was building huge trucks. As part of the requirements, they showed us the whole assembly line from the time they receive the material till the time the whole truck comes out. It was a huge plant. Everything from chassis, engine, and cab were all in the assembly line. A single stop meant the whole line would be stopped, delaying the production of the truck.

When we saw the final truck coming out of the line, I asked the manager if I could see how it is inside the cab, behind the wheel, and see how it felt to drive a huge thing. He agreed and I went and sat inside. I felt how I might feel if I was driving the truck. That was the last time I had that nightmare.

That's fascinating. It's as if you faced the fear head-on and the fear resolved.

Much later, I had the same kind of incident. I used to have nightmares where there would be people in our house for a party. The house would be filled with people. I would think that the party is over and try to get them out. But they would come back in. They would come in from windows as I pushed them out through the door. Until I woke up with a sweat. That dream continued until my viral load became undetectable and then I never had that nightmare again.

It's like our minds attempt to work out our troubles in our sleep.

I think if I had not gone in the direction of engineering, I might have become interested in brain science. I did my master's thesis in artificial intelligence (AI). In my second year of my master's degree, we had to select a thesis. Being in computer science, AI really intrigued me. There was a professor, Dr. Sembugamoorthy, who was doing research in the field. I asked him for guidance. He told me that he is studying how a child in preschool learns the language without knowing the grammar, syntax, or even nouns. I could, if I wanted, extend his model to handle the time aspect. For instance: John went to school after he had breakfast.

I agreed, and commenced the thesis. After working on it for a year, it was time to present it to a committee of three professors, including my guide, and two of the professors were external to the project. My presentation went very well. After the presentation, in the question and answers phase, they asked me why my method was better than a competitor's method. I had thought about the competitor's method and found it to be a better representation. But my thesis was within the parameters of my guide's research.

I told them that I had simply extended his static sentences to dynamic sentences. This satisfied the external professor and they gave me an A+ grade. But, my guide was not happy with my answer, so he refused to sign it.

After the presentation, I had only one week before I left for the USA. So, I left without completing my M. Tech. degree. My friend later had the guide sign it (he gave me a C grade) and I had my degree awarded next year.

You said you might have chosen to go into brain science. You still could. There are plenty of unsolved problems and mysteries about the brain and about human behavior.

I'm definitely interested in learning more about psychology and therapy.

I should give you a book to read. Let me find it. Here it is. *The Gift of Therapy* by Irvin Yalom.

This will give me some good reading material for my vacation. I'm going on a cruise for a couple weeks with Joe. We leave next week. That reminds me: after next week's session, I won't see you for the following two weeks.

A cruise with Joe sounds great. I'm glad you have something to look forward to. And, I'll be very interested to hear your thoughts about *The Gift of Therapy*.

Nine

I finished reading the book you gave me last week. It was very interesting. Maybe you have another one I can read on the cruise next week?

Of course. Tell me what you found interesting about *The Gift of Therapy*.

It helped me better understand what you have been up to for the past few months.

And what did you discover? What have I been up to?

I made some notes. In Chapter 10, he writes that the therapist must create a new therapy for each client. I see that you have done this with me. You have twenty-nine other clients and you have told me at many times that our interaction is unique.

Yes, I think that's true. Each client is different and you are such a unique individual. I have never met anyone like you before. And, your situation is unlike any other client I have had before. So, our therapeutic approach must be unique as well.

He also writes quite a bit about empathy. In Chapter 6, he wrote about the need for the therapist to "look through the client's window" and accept him as he is. And, I think you've tried to do that from the beginning.

Empathy is the heart of therapy in many ways. You say that I've *tried* to do that. That suggests that you feel that I've not always succeeded in my empathy with you.

Well, I mean that you've tried to understand my reasons for wanting to end my life, but you are limited in your ability to empathize with me and accept me and my wishes by your professional standards.

That's definitely a paradox. I've always found it strange that, as a psychologist, I'm supposed to honor all of the decisions of my clients, except for one. When someone says they want to kill themself, I'm supposed to try to prevent this. Everyone who sees me knows this. I tell them this the first time we meet just as I told you; I say that one of the only exceptions to the confidentiality I must maintain as a psychologist is if a person is in imminent danger of hurting themselves.

And, I understand that it's a requirement of your profession. It's just ironic that it's applied across the board with no consideration of the individual circumstances.

It's implicit in the contract of coming to see me that I will try to help keep my clients alive. I've met many people who

were legitimately suicidal, who expressed very real, very scary thoughts of wanting to die. I've always done whatever I could to keep them alive. When I agreed to work with you, Vishwas, that was my intention. You asked me to help you find reasons to live and a new zest for living. Every week I see you, I'm trying to think of what will give you that zest and reason for living.

And there's no doubt it has been working. But it hasn't been as simple as finding reasons to live. Except that I look forward to our time together, and to some sense, that's a reason to keep living.

This other passage in the book made me think about it differently. In Chapter 11, he writes, "The patients' views of helpful events in therapy are generally relational, often involving some act of the therapist that stretched outside the frame of therapy or some graphic example of the therapist's consistency and presence."

It reminded me of several things that you did that went over and above what I might expect of a therapist.

Such as?

When you stopped and got me the information about volunteering with the gay youth organization. And, when you encouraged me to write my memoirs and you offered to transcribe my speaking, it was such a surprise to me that you could actually understand what I was saying.

So, I get props for my stenography!

Ha-ha!

When you first came to me, Vishwas, I had a conversation about you with my former advisor whom I have great respect for, and also with my best friend. I shared your situation with them and I told them about your wish to end your life. We talked quite a bit and after talking to them, I decided that I was going to do whatever I can to keep you alive as long as you are my client.

It's interesting. You made that clear right from the start, and yet back then, I felt that you were more inclined to let me go at the time of my choosing. You seemed to really understand my feelings about it and I thought you were telling me what your profession required you to say. And since then, it became clear that you were not going to let me go on my terms.

There's no doubt I was conflicted in my feelings about your wishes to end your life. But I decided to trust the process. The process that my mentors have told me to believe in, and the process that I've told my own mentees to believe in. Faith in the idea that, if I allow myself to join another person, if I allow that person to open himself to me, that eventually we'll figure something out together that will allow him to feel better.

I appreciate that you have been very open and vulnerable with me in a way that I imagine you are not with most patients. In this

98

book, he writes quite a bit about revealing your own personal life and about being transparent with your clients.

Most of what he writes on that subject is cautionary against being *too* transparent and exposing too much of your personal life.

But right from the beginning, what I learned about your personal life endeared you to me. When I saw online that you were married to a Black woman and that you had a best friend who is gay, I felt that you were someone I could connect with. And, you've often shared other personal aspects of your life with me. All of that has helped me to build a closer bond with you.

I'm glad those things helped you feel more comfortable with me, but do you mind if I ask, how did you find that information about me?

On Facebook. I could only see certain pictures because we have one friend in common and your privacy settings allow friends of friends to see some items.

Who is our common friend?

Scott Lewallen.

I've known Scott since my college days. I went to my first gay bar with Scott. Small world.

I also saw a post about you dropping your best friend at the airport from a psychologist conference. Somehow, I figured out he was gay and also a psychologist.

I have to tell you, Vishwas, that you continue to astound me. You are such a unique person with such a wonderful perspective, and such a vibrant personality. You have had such an extraordinary curiosity. Not to mention your intellect and your passion for life and that drive that has literally kept you alive.

You said a moment ago that you think that therapy is working for you. Does this mean you are thinking less about ending your life?

Yes, I haven't had many thoughts about suicide for a while. And I really look forward to our conversations each week. Joe noticed it, too. He said I'm talking more about the future and making plans than I have for quite some time. I told him, "This is Vishwas 3.0" and we had a good laugh. You remember that Vishwas 2.0 was when my viral load went to zero.

That makes me very happy to hear that. You seem to be different, too. You seem more peaceful and content.

I think that's true. And I think it really helps to have an interest. I really enjoyed reading the book you gave me and I look forward to learning more about how therapy works. It's still a bit of a mystery.

And I think you like a mystery, right? You like the challenge of figuring things out.

I think I've always been a very curious person and you're right—I always like to figure things out. I tend to lose interest once I understand how things work. This has happened throughout my life. When I was in college, I became the chess champion and the bridge doubles champion, but then I lost interest in both of them. Once I knew how it works, I lost interest.

So, solving the mystery is the thing for you. I know you approached your HIV as a puzzle to be solved. I'm sure that worked in your career as well, right?

Oh, I certainly thrived on solving puzzles in my work. I always focused on finding ways things could work.

When we were talking last week about your career, I meant to ask you something. Did you ever come out to your coworkers?

Not until I went to work for CBIS, which was the last company I worked for before I went on disability. Well, DynCorp bought CBIS before I left, so that was the last company I worked for.

Until then, I was only out to a few individuals—mostly other gay people. Back in 1991 (the same year I met Joe), I came out to one former coworker, Kirk Carpenter. I was still working for Unisys.

That's where you were on the track to become a VP?

Yes, and where I did the Quest proposal for the billion-dollar project. I worked on several other projects for Unisys, including one that led to a big court battle. We were competing against another company and found out they cheated on their bid. It involved explaining to our lawyers and the judges about how the computers worked, in simple terms. We won the suit. Then, the client, the Florida Department of Law Enforcement, told us they canceled the contract for budgetary reasons. But, we think they were pissed off because of the lawsuit.

Anyway, I never came out at any of my workplaces up to that point. Then my colleague Kirk Carpenter left Unisys to work for another company. He asked me if I would like to come work with him. I asked him if we could talk about it over a drink.

We met at a bar and he told me that he was now a VP with a company called Cincinnati Bell and wanted me to go with him. We talked about the job. I told him I don't want a high-pressure job anymore. I just want to be a programmer. This was when I had become aware that my T-cells were declining with each project I took on.

He said that he wanted me in that capacity as a programmer and that it didn't have to be as stressful. Then, I said that he had to match the same salary I was getting at Unisys. I didn't tell him why, but I needed to pay for my medication, which was quite expensive. He agreed to pay me the same.

I wanted to go with him, but I didn't want to have this disease hanging over my head. Apart from my doctors and other gay co-workers I discovered along the way, this would be the first time I was coming out to a colleague. So, I decided to tell him that I was HIV-positive and I could die as soon as one year.

Kirk said, "If I get six months of you on the project, I will have my money's worth. And you being gay doesn't bother me."

So, you got exactly what you wanted and you were out as well.

Yes. Well, I started writing code as we agreed, but my talent didn't stay hidden long, and soon they made me the "chief scientist" at Dyncorp.

And we had some interesting projects there. One project was to implement systems for a correctional institution in Dayton, Ohio. I got to go to the prison and learn how it works.

You are certainly interested in how things work, and I think the more complicated the system is, the greater your interest.

Yes. That's true. Perhaps that's why psychology is interesting to me.

Oh, that reminds me, I want to give you another book to read. Here is *The Heart and Soul of Change*. It's by a group of therapists and I think you will appreciate the research they discuss about what works in therapy and why it works when it works.

That does sound very interesting. I will take it along on the cruise although I don't know if I'll get a lot of reading done. Joe and I will be with a couple of our best friends and a ship full of gay men.

Well, I'm sure you'll have a great time. And we'll see you again in three weeks, right?

Yes. We'll be gone for two weeks so I'll be missing those two sessions.

Bon voyage, Vishwas!

Ten

Happy New Year, Vishwas. And welcome back. How was your cruise?

It was not what I had expected. It was disappointing. I almost didn't come to this appointment, but Joe insisted that I see you.

So sorry to hear that about the cruise. I'm glad Joe convinced you to come. I missed you the last couple weeks. I truly look forward to seeing you each week, Vishwas. Do you want to tell me about the cruise?

To begin with, I was the guy in a wheelchair on a gay cruise, so I didn't meet anyone to have sex with. Then I got sick and I was miserable. It was some kind of stomach infection. I shit myself and Joe had to be my nursemaid.

That's awful, Vishwas. It's good Joe was there to care for you.

No, I don't want Joe to have to clean up after me and do everything for me. I am still not able to function on my own. And it isn't just on the cruise. I hate it when Joe does things for me in the morning. I hate it when Joe has to prepare me for the shower and dress

105

me afterward. I hate it that Joe has to do all the cooking for me. I hate it when Joe has to take me to all my appointments. It's not me. I don't want to continue life like this.

I'm so sorry for all this pain you are experiencing, Vishwas. Are you having thoughts again about ending your life?

Yes.

I'm so sorry to hear that. You were feeling so much better just three weeks ago.

I think our sessions have been very helpful and meaningful. You've helped me to reflect on my life and all that I've accomplished and enjoyed in spite of the HIV and challenges.

I've looked at these achievements of my past life and I consider the level of effort it's going to take to return to the life I lost since the stroke. It seems to me I've had a good sixty years of my life. Why don't I call it quits? The people who love me will be hurt by my departure. But, their sorrow will be the same if I die today or next year or in ten years.

It sounds like all the pain and struggle resulting from your stroke has come to a head.

Originally, Joe asked me to wait for six months before I made that decision. Later, it became one year and then two years.

106

Now the two years are over. I am still not able to function on my own.

How does Joe feel about all this? About caring for you as he does?

He says it's okay for him. I know he loves me and he wants the best for me. In a way, the stroke has taken a toll on our relationship, though you won't find it in our attitude toward each other. We are still very much in love.

But it has changed the dynamic between us. Before the stroke, I was a very outgoing, type-A personality, and Joe was a shy, intro-verted person. The stroke has caused a role reversal, and we both find it very difficult to get used to.

After the cruise, the topic of suicide came up again. I asked Joe again and he finally (very, very reluctantly) gave me his blessing. It's simple now; I can choose next month, next year or never, but it would be my choice.

Ultimately, it has always been your choice to live or take your life.

Yes, but a very, very tough choice. A choice no one else really un-derstands or supports.

I even looked at taking the issue up to the American Psychology Association. I watched a few videos about the subject. For 99.99

percent of their clients, the rule makes sense. But, I am a special case. I shouldn't be stuck in the middle of the psychology business on this.

For the simple principle of the thing, I know I am making it much bigger than it is, and for what reason? Just to say that I got the thing I wanted in my way?

And I'm very concerned about how it would impact you and your practice.

How do you mean that?

I have involved you in this. I wonder all the time, *How would this affect your psychologist's business?* The one thing I don't want to do is do any harm. When I told you I thought about not coming to see you today, it was because of this. I thought if I ended my therapy and then gave it some time before I made my decision, it would not reflect on you.

I'm honored by your concern for me. It reassures me that what we're doing here is going in the right direction. We are building a deep connection with each other.

Yes. We have a real connection. I have looked forward to seeing you every week. You have become the high point of my life. Losing your contact is the last thing I want to do.

108

By the way, I read most of the book you gave me, and one of the interesting things they said was that the "therapist effect" on the outcome of therapy has mostly to do with the quality of the relationship between the therapist and the client and how they feel about each other. I found that interesting.

That is quite interesting. And as I recall, the research shows that the "therapist effect" is a very small part of the overall effectiveness of therapy.

Yes, 87 percent of the variance has to do with what is going on in the life of the client. And less than 1 percent of the variance has to do with the therapeutic model. In fact, they call therapy the "placebo delivery." I feel that the placebo effect is undervalued. In double-blind medical studies, they ignore the placebo part. But in psychology, the placebo is the main part.

That's a very good point. It goes back to what we talked about the first day we met. Do you remember?

I'm sure it was significant, but I'm going to have to blame it on my stroke. I'm sorry, I don't remember.

I said therapy can serve as a replacement for the intimate relationships that are missing in modern society.

I think they wrote something about that in this book, too.

And I think we both agree that this part is working between us very well.

I agree. By the way, when I told you about not wanting to see you again, it wasn't that I didn't want to see you. On the cruise, I thought many times of things I was looking forward to sharing with you and discussing with you. It was really about not wanting you to be affected by my decision to commit suicide if I decided to go through with it.

I'm glad you decided to come back.

Thank Joe for that.

I will. Is he here with you today?

Yes, he always brings me and usually sits out in the lobby.

I'll be sure to speak to him today when we're done. You know, we really haven't spoken much about Joe. You mentioned that the dynamic of your relationship has shifted since your stroke, but you haven't really told me that much about your life together. I don't even know how you met.

I met Joe in a bar in 1991.

Tell me about it.

At that point, I wasn't frequenting the bars, but we had just been to Justin's younger brother's wedding and we decided to go out. I had just had my knee surgery and we all went back to my place. I was quite attracted to Joe and he seemed to be interested in me, but for the next few months, it was only by my initiative that we saw each other. He didn't contact me and sometimes, he didn't respond to my phone calls.

We planned to meet for dinner on New Year's Eve, 1991, and that night, he told me he was in the air force. He had been stationed at Andrews Air Force Base and now he was going to be deployed to Saudi Arabia. After he left, I realized he didn't leave his address with me, so I did quite a bit of research and found an address for him in Saudi Arabia. I wrote him a postcard and kept it very friendly, careful not to expose that he was gay. This was before Don't Ask, Don't Tell, and being gay was grounds for discharge from the military.

Joe wrote back to me and we carried on a correspondence until he returned three months later. When he landed, he came right to my place and we began our romantic relationship. On the second date after he returned, we both acknowledged that we were falling in love. As we were confessing our love for each other, Joe said he had a secret to share with me. I told him I had something to share with him as well.

He took out his wallet and handed me his military ID card. I asked, "Why are you showing this to me?" He told me to look at it closely. He pointed to a box that contained the word *Chaplain*. I asked him if that was his secret.

"I'm a chaplain in the air force," he said, "It's my job. And I'm a Catholic priest." He looked worried, like he expected me to run out of the restaurant.

"So, you're a chaplain and I'm a programmer." I said, "What's the difference? It's no big deal to me." He reached out and grabbed my hand on top of the table. I could see that he was relieved.

Joe told me that before he joined the air force as a chaplain, he had been a parish priest for eleven years. He said that in the past, when he told guys he was a priest, they would immediately run away or start acting strangely about it. I assured him I wasn't going to run away and it didn't matter to me that he was a priest.

He asked me what I wanted to tell him and I shared with him that I was HIV-positive, that I had just stopped taking AZT, and that no other treatment was available at that time.

He told me, "It doesn't matter because we are in love." He made an effort to reassure me that we could still be together.

That's beautiful.

What can I say about Joe? He is the life source for me. Over the past thirty years, he has always been my anchor. He went through ups and downs in my life. He gave me the encouragement to live. He never once said no to me. Without him, I cannot imagine living so long. The credit for my survival goes to Joe. It's like two individuals who are tied by some string but are free to live their own lives. In the last thirty years, we had only one fight. He is very active in the church and I am an atheist. People find this to be an unusual combination. But somehow, it works very nicely for us.

So, you've really had two great loves in your life. Justin and Joe.

Yes. I have been lucky.

And I'm assuming by some of what you've told me that your relationship with Joe was also an open relationship?

Yes. It's funny how that began. I went to his apartment one evening to surprise him. He had given me a key, so I let myself in. I thought he would be home, but he wasn't there. After waiting a couple of hours, I went into the bedroom and fell asleep.

About one in the morning, I heard him stumbling into the house. He was talking before he came into the room and I assumed he was talking to me. Then I remembered he didn't know I was there. So, who is he talking to? He walked into the bedroom and I said, "I came to surprise you."

"Oh, wait a minute," he said and he started walking out of the room. I heard him speaking again in a low voice, saying something like,

"You have to go. My lover is here." Then he came right back in, apologizing to me, "I'm so sorry. I'll tell you how it happened."

I said, "No, no. I'm sleeping now. Let me sleep and you go and have sex with him in the living room." So, he left and I fell back asleep.

At some point, he came back into the room and slept with me. When we woke up in the morning, Joe realized he was running late for work, but he had promised to drive the other guy to the train station. I told him, "You go to work and I'll drive him."

That evening, we talked and agreed to have an open relationship.

And this wasn't your first cruise together, was it?

Oh, no. There have been many cruises. Joe and I went on our first cruise together in 1993. It was a gay cruise and we thought it was wonderful being together in the Caribbean with a hundred other gay men. It was during that first cruise that Joe got a phone call from his officer informing him he had made the rank of major in the air force. That same year, Joe was deployed to Bitburg, Germany. He was stationed there for two years.

Were you able to go with him?

I didn't live with him there, of course. But during that time, I was able to take seven trips to visit him and he came back home on leave five times. On my trips, we would travel together. We had a wonderful time in Paris and drove around France.

Another time, we visited England and Ireland, which is where Joe's ancestors lived. I suggested that we go visit the places his ancestors lived. Joe was quite shy, and at the time, he was still closeted, so I did most of the research and made most of the contacts. It turned out to be a wonderful experience.

On another trip, we visited Amsterdam and we had a delightful vacation in The Netherlands. The interesting thing I remember is that, in all my travels, only three times my bag was checked by the customs. Twice when I had been to The Netherlands, once when I had been to Tokyo. Probably, they suspected that I brought some illegal drugs. Obviously, I was cleared.

You mentioned Joe was stationed for two years in Germany. Did he come back here then?

No. That's when he was stationed next at Abilene, Texas.

I remember that was where you had trouble finding a doctor.

Yes. That was in 1995. It was the year Justin died. I cried a lot. That was when my doctor recommended that I go on disability. I decided to sell my house and just travel wherever Joe was stationed.

But that's not what ended up happening, right?

Right. I hadn't sold my house, so I just traveled every couple weeks between Abilene and Virginia. I was able to get better care in Virginia. And by the next year, when I was very ill and it seemed like I was not going to get better, Joe decided to quit the air force to enjoy whatever time I had left with me. He forfeited his pension and lost all his benefits.

That's quite a love story, Vishwas. I really want you to write a memoir. I want to give you a very special book to read this week. It's one of the classics of my profession: *On Becoming a Person* by Carl Rogers.

I look forward to reading it and I'll see you next week.

Eleven

I'm so happy to see you today, Vishwas.

More than any other time?

Yes. I was really worried about you. The cruise really left you in distress.

The cruise put all of my limitations in front of me. Everything I can't do since the stroke. But in time, I'll only remember the good parts of it. Anyway, I had to come see you at the very least to return your book.

Did you find it interesting? I gave you the book by Carl Rogers, right?

Yes. It got me thinking about many things. I realized that throughout my life, I have mentally inoculated myself against many things. But I never inoculated myself against a stroke.

Mentally inoculated? Against what sort of things?

When I was in college, I would think about all the things that can happen in the future such as finishing school and getting married and how the married life would look like. And what raising children will look like. Then how the midlife crisis will happen. Then when the actual thing happened, I would handle it better.

Walk me through it. How did it work?

For instance: midlife crisis. When I was quite young, before I experienced a midlife crisis, I imagined that I had accomplished all my goals and I had a midlife crisis. For a few days, typically two or three, I would feel the anxiety and depression of "Why I am doing the things I do?", "What is the meaning of it?", "What do I do now that half of my life is over?", "What do I do to return to my youth?" Then I would come to a realization and return to my previous self.

If you consider all the situations that you might encounter and have an answer to all, you develop the quality of *sthitaprajna*, or centered.

You've mentioned this *sthitaprajna* before. Am I saying it right?

Yes. Sthi-ta-pra-jna.

My mother used to say, "You can be whoever you want, but I want you to become *sthitaprajna*." This means "centered," "stoic," or "one who is not affected by good or bad fortunes."

It sounds like a core value for you.

That's why I called my company Centered Systems.

That makes sense. It's simple but meaningful.

I got the domains Centered.com and centeredsystems.com and I got several offers to buy them for up to $50k, but I never entertained the offers.

Mental inoculation seems related in some way to how you disassociated from things and people when you thought you were dying. Both seem to deal with fear of the unknown.

That is an insightful observation. "Mental inoculation" and "disassociation with living" are two main features of *sthitaprajna*, or being a centered person. But they are not the same.

Mental inoculation is finding a solution to a difficult situation before the situation arises. And so, I inoculated all the possible things that I could think of happening in this life.

Disassociation from living is a practice for facing death.

For dealing with one's fear of death?

Yes. If we are going to die at some point, then why are we afraid of dying? The reason is due to our liking of physical things or people. These are good things to have. But if we are dying for sure, then it helps to slowly disassociate from such things. That is what I did in 1986 when I was diagnosed with HIV, and again in 1996, 2006, and 2016 each time I faced imminent death.

It's interesting that those events are ten years apart.

I never noticed that. Maybe we see what happens in 2026! Ha-ha.

And when I dissociated all that stuff, the important thing is then I'm not afraid of dying. Dying just becomes the next step with no other significance. But when I reassociate with everything, then dying becomes far away.

But in 2016, when I had a stroke, my left brain was gone and so I had trouble reassociating with those things. I felt a gap between past me and present me.

What sort of a gap?

It's really hard to describe how it happened, but I had a disconnect between the past me and the present me. And the disconnect was like, "Who is this guy?" And, "Who are these people around you?" In my mind, it was not coming together. After some period of time, then it came together.

And as you say, a stroke is what you never inoculated yourself for even though you were able to prepare yourself for everything else including death.

Yes. But stroke is like a half-death. I wasn't prepared for that and I didn't know how to do that at the time.

I don't know how you would have done that. If I'm understanding this, you would go through the experience in your mind like a chess player imagining the next moves. By imagining yourself living through these experiences?

Yes, I imagine going through these experiences and then I would come out of that in a day or so with the understanding of how that works. It's like a partially disabled virus that gets injected into your system and you develop antibodies that help you fight the real virus, if you get it.

That's fascinating, Vishwas. In each of these situations, you had to engage your imagination. You had to be curious to find whatever is challenging and interesting about it.

Yes, but I had to be *more* than curious. I had to live through the experience.

And each of these situations was like a puzzle or a challenge to your mind. Is it possible that you haven't gotten curious about the stroke? This half-death as you put it?

No, I'm sure I haven't. But the main thing about this situation is that I don't have all the equipment I had before the stroke. I am a different person after the stroke.

I hear you. But, it seems that some of your essential qualities such as curiosity are still very much alive in post-stroke Vishwas.

And if you look carefully at the challenges you have faced in your life, curiosity was the key to conquering each of them. It's kind of the story of your life. You would face a challenge and get curious and go to work. It's the throughline in battling HIV and also in your career. It's why they put you in the "High Potential" group. You're unstoppable in the face of a challenge.

What you're saying is true of my life before the stroke. Even when I was in the HiPo program, apparently it wasn't challenging enough for me.

How so?

Have I told you about JEDA—the program I created to help judges sort through conflicting evidence?

I don't think so.

When I was in HiPo, I mentioned to my friend Chuck Rippey that it really wasn't all that challenging for me. He was an administrative law judge for the Department of Labor, and he told me about a problem he had with black lung diseases. The laws were so intertwined over the years that it was difficult to determine when a person is legally disabled. I agreed to work on it with him.

I studied the laws regarding black lung cases. It occurred to me that it would be complex, but doable for an expert system in computers to do this. So, I developed a program called "JEDA:" Judicial Expert Decisional Aide using Prolog. The program did everything by the law, and when it came to the decision point, it asked the judge to make a decision and justify it. The program did everything else including printing the decision.

Sounds like artificial intelligence.

It was. Using this program, Chuck was able to handle five times the number of cases. Then he tried to get other judges in the labor department to use the program including the chief judge. And this is where the snag appeared. The chief judge was too afraid of the implication. He felt like the computers were making a decision and soon his job would no longer be required. Also, the judges didn't type on the computers. They had the secretary do it for them.

A prominent journal on AI and law invited Chuck and me to present at their conference in Vancouver, Canada. The audience was quite interested. We had a great trip to Canada.

Chuck got several years of service out of that program. But it didn't catch on with other judges.

Sounds like you were ahead of your time.

You're right. This spring, yet another journal article cited JEDA as an early example of AI applications in the courts.

I'm sure you found yourself ahead of your time at other points in your career and life.

Yes, I did. In 1990, I was on a project that required a network of Windows computers that would do word processing, spreadsheets, and such. But, it saved everything on a central server on the big mainframe computer.

I came up with an idea of Windows-based software that would back up the files to the mainframe in the background. It would make the solution much cheaper. The Unisys people in charge turned down the idea. And, I thought their decision was a mistake because it had great potential to save computing time and money.

On vacation to Justin's family, I took a programming book and my laptop and built this software. (In 1990, the laptops were quite limited and very bulky.) The company didn't want anything to do with it and gave me a no-conflict certificate.

Previously, when I went to Vancouver to present the JEDA application, I created my company I told you about (called Centered Systems) so I could expense the trip. I used the company again to sell this program.

I would sell this through CompuServe, a few copies each month. I called this "Second Copy." This is before the Internet as we know it today. In 1996, after I retired on disability, I worked on it to keep my mind busy. I kept upgrading it.

Suddenly, reporters started to recommend it, and it even got recommended by Microsoft and Intel. With the exposure came success. We never promoted the software and kept the price to be $29.95 (which continues till this day in version 9.0). Money started rolling in.

This happened in 1996? Isn't that when Joe quit the air force and moved back to Virginia?

Yes. Joe had just retired and moved in with me to take care of me while I was dying. I published the first version of Second Copy in 1991. But I rewrote it in Delphi in 1996.

I didn't want to lose my disability, so Joe and I formed a partnership and sold the software through him while making me a silent partner. Over the years, Second Copy received seven annual software awards. Now, it's still going, but at a much lower rate.

I wondered how you survived since Joe left the air force. So that became Joe's next career?

Well, when Joe first came back from Texas to Virginia, he did some substitute teaching in a "gifted" student program in a high school. He didn't care for it much. He said being a substitute teacher was like being a glorified babysitter.

Joe had told me that, when he was young, he knew he wanted to be a priest or a lawyer. I suggested to him that he had time now to get his law degree. He was fifty at the time and he did it. He studied at George Mason and passed the bar. He opened his own practice and set up our company and managed our legal matters.

That's amazing. And in the middle of all of this, you took lots of cruises.

Yes. We loved cruises. We even went on a cruise to nowhere.

Sounds intriguing.

It was just after I became undetectable in 2006. We left from Baltimore toward Bermuda. A hurricane came up and we had to go out to sea away from the hurricane. The ship's radar was not working properly so we were out at sea and never stopped at any ports until we came back to port in Baltimore.

So, you stayed on the ship the whole time?

Yes. We were at sea for five days. The company gave us 50 percent off, and because the radar failed, they gave us a voucher for 25 percent off a future trip.

We went on a Mediterranean cruise in 2008, with our friends Patrick and Steve. It was two and a half weeks and we visited Spain, France, Dubrovnik Yugoslavia, and Italy. I remember I was shopping in Florence and our friends told us to hurry to catch our bus. I was using a cane, but we made it back just in time.

It sounds like you had some wonderful adventures on these cruises.

We did. On one cruise we took to Cozumel, we went with our friends Chuck and Sig, and also my brother and his wife and daughter came with us.

We also met our friends Amit and Kenny on cruises. Well, I met Kenny originally through another dating app in 2012. He was texting me from somewhere, and eventually, I realized that he is working and living on a ship.

We went on chatting and he told me about his special friend in England who wanted to develop an application for the iPhone. He asked if I would talk to him. I said, yes, and I talked to Amit. Then after a while, it became clear that he's not going to become a programmer, but we became friends. And then he said that he had seen Kenny only once before in England, when Kenny was onshore.

So, there was one chance that he could take to meet Kenny off the ship, but his visa was just about to expire. So, I said we can go, and Joe and I decided to go on this cruise. We checked with Kenny, and we booked the cruise for twelve days. There was only one cabin left. So, Joe and I took that room.

Kenny was working and Amit was staying in his room below the deck. So, we got to learn a lot more about how life is above the deck and below the deck. Every time we got into port, Kenny got out with us because his manager let him go. We started from Athens and went on to the Greek Isles and Istanbul. Then after that, we ended up in Venice, Italy, just one day before Amit's visa expired. So, he went directly to the airport. Then Joe and I spent some time in Venice.

Three months later, Kenny had a shore-leave. Then he connected up again with Amit and they decided to become partners. They are now married and they live in the UK. And we make sure that we meet at least once a year and we talk every week.

It sounds like you have a wonderful network of friends.

I do. We have wonderful friends. I have to tell you about a cruise we got to go on for free.

Why am I not surprised? When you write that memoir of yours, you'll have to call it *The Voyages of Vishwas*. No—*The Amazing Voyages of Vishwas*.

Once I discovered that my viral load was undetectable and I knew I will live a long time, my attention went to my favorite topic: computers. Back in 2001, when I had lymphoma and had a long time to think, I came up with an idea that would let gay people find each other based on their location. I called this "Proximate."

Clever name. Proxi-Mate. Ha-ha.

At the time, the technology was not there yet. In 2007, when the first iPhone was introduced, I immediately bought it. I remember standing in line with all the other excited buyers. In 2008, when Apple introduced a way to program for it on Macintosh computers, I bought myself a MacBook. I got familiar with it as I had with the Windows computers. I got my first app called "MisCalculator" on the iPhone. Over time, I had eleven applications in the App Store.

Then in 2009, I came across an app for gay people called Grindr.

Grindr? Is this how you know Scott?

Yes. So, as you know, Scott and Joel were cofounders of Grindr. Joel did the marketing and Scott did the design parts. Grindr—similar to my idea of Proximate—would find other gay people in your vicinity. I was excited about this. I started using it. Then in mid-2009, there was an ad on Grindr that they were looking for an iPhone programmer. I immediately wrote to them about my programming skills and desire to work with the app.

In the beginning, they gave me a task to work on localization strings. Then it slowly moved into writing code for metric to imperial units. Then I worked on putting ads, called Mobclix, in the program. Then language translation, to speed up the "load more guys" feature and other features. By this time, they recognized my skills. I became a part of the development team. On Grindr at the time, there were three developers: there was a guy in Boston, one in Costa Rica, and me in Washington, DC.

But I was doing this work for free. There was no compensation or money exchange for my work. The founder of Grindr, Joel Simkhai, asked me several times. He wanted to pay me. I was on disability, and if I worked, then my disability would stop. When disability stops, my private insurance would also stop. My disease would come back any-time and I could not afford that. It would mean the end.

And you probably couldn't handle a full-time job at that point.

Probably not. So, I hired a lawyer and tried to negotiate an agree-ment with the insurance company. But it didn't work. So, I decid-ed to not accept any payment for it. Joel felt uncomfortable, but understood my situation. I did it for the challenge and to be part of something that made life better for gay men.

In 2010, the iPad came out. It offered a big screen and a lot more room for the applications. I immediately decided to make Grindr work on that, as an iPad app and not an iPhone app. I wrote the Grindr app to work on iPad in the next four months. Then Joel and Scott sent Joe and me on an Atlantis cruise to Mexico, all ex-penses paid including the airfare.

The cruise was very nice. Atlantis is a gay travel agency and the whole ship was filled with gay people. We had been to Mexico before; Joe and I had spent a week in Acapulco and I had been to Mexico City and Puerto Vallarta with Justin before that. But this cruise was different. A ship filled with two thousand guys means "party all the time."

I continued to work on Grindr and started to work on Blendr, the straight version of Grindr. Then Joel and Scott flew us back to California for the release of the Blendr party. By then, Grindr had received some large investors and Joel had hired a large staff. In 2011, it went from our three-person development team to one hundred people. They asked me to join the team in Los Angeles. But I had to turn them down. That brought my involvement with Grindr to an end. But I remained a good friend of Joel and Scott.

And it must be satisfying knowing that you made this contribution to the gay community.

Well, I didn't really publicize that I was the initial developer of Grindr. But one time, Joe and I were at a party and I mentioned to someone that I was the initial writer of Grindr and the guy bowed in front of me and he laid down on the ground and touched the ground with his forehead like he was worshiping and he said, "You have saved so many lives."

That's hilarious!

I'm sure my work on Grindr hasn't really saved lives. Not like your psychology work does.

Well, thank you, and I'm sure your work *has* made a difference in many people's lives.

And on that subject, let me give you another psychology book that I think you will find interesting. It's *The Healing Connection* by Jean Baker Miller. We have to keep feeding your curiosity about therapy.

I am enjoying reading these books. Then sometimes, I wonder if these books are your way to keep me coming back. You know if you lend me a book, I will bring it back to you.

Ha-ha. Maybe they do both: they keep your curiosity engaged *and* they keep you coming back. Vishwas, you know what I find remarkable about you?

What is that?

In spite of all the illness and difficulties you have endured and the struggles you continue to encounter after your stroke, you have somehow managed to maintain a great sense of humor and also to have a wonderful life full of truly amazing friends and experiences.

I think it's because when I look back in my life, I don't remember the difficulties, only the wonderful moments and people.

You are still very much the Gay Crow.

Ha-ha. I guess that's true.

Twelve

That was an interesting book you gave me to read.

Did you like it?

It was mostly about relationships.

Yes, relationships and psychology. I thought you might find that interesting.

Yes. Mostly, it emphasizes the importance of relationships for healthy psychology and also in therapy. It's very similar in philosophy to a couple of the other books I've read. I can see how these have influenced your approach to therapy.

This one puts even more emphasis on relationships. The first book I read said that the relationship between therapist and client counts for less than 15 percent of the outcome. And 85 percent of the outcome of therapy is determined by what happens in the life of the patient. Or client.

I'm sure that's accurate. However, within the sphere of the therapeutic process, the quality of the relationship is more important than other aspects of the therapy.

Yes. I think they said the therapeutic approach accounted for less than 1 percent of the outcome.

So, what does all this mean for you, Vishwas?

I agree that the relationship is the most important.

Something you said last time got me thinking about our relationship. You joked that I am giving you these books to read as an enticement to come back. You don't really think that, do you?

Sometimes I think that, but I'm also finding the books interesting.

You know when you first came to see me, you were looking to me to help you find or rediscover your "zest" for living, but you did everything in your power to convince me that it was alright for you to end your life. It really felt like it was "on me" to keep you alive. It's my job, of course, but at times, it felt like an awful burden.

And I felt like we were making progress. We were definitely bonding. I was bonding with you at least. I've never met anyone like you and I grew to care deeply about you.

Then you came back from that cruise and it seemed like we were starting over. Joe gave you his consent to end your life if you chose to, but again, he asked you to talk to me about it. And it was "on me" again to keep you alive.

I'm sorry if I gave you the impression that we were back to the beginning. I don't feel that way.

Well, I was more concerned that you felt somehow manipulated into coming back by my giving you the books on psychology. I'm convinced that the key to rediscovering your zest for life will come from you getting curious and intrigued by a new challenge and I sensed you were developing that kind of interest in psychology and therapy.

I am finding the books interesting and it could become the challenge that will bring me that zest for life I have been missing.

So, what about this idea that I'm just getting you to come back with the books?

If I really think about it, I'm coming back because of you. And our relationship. You are the most intellectually stimulating person in my life. And even though I don't have the intellect I once had, this is still important to me.

As for the psychology books, we'll see where that goes. Three things come to mind about this study of psychology. One, in some ways, it seems like more of a diversion than a new challenge.

Diversion? How is that?

It's like they said about 85 percent of the outcome of therapy has to do with what's going on in the client's life. And in my life, that has to do with my recovery from my stroke. I would say that everything hinges on my recovering the use of my leg and hand. I don't think my mind is coming back, but there is some noticeable progress in my body.

You say, "Everything hinges" on that. Does that mean whether you continue to want to end your life depends on your progress recovering from the stroke?

It definitely does. I think I'm willing to shelve the issue of ending my life for now. And so, we are sort of creating a distraction while I very gradually recover from my stroke.

Because your further recovery is what will make the biggest difference with respect to your desire to keep living?

Yes.

And what's the second point you wanted to make about the psychology books?

The second point is that I would like to discuss psychology more with you. I prefer that to talking on and on about my past experiences.

Fair enough. I'm happy to discuss psychology with you although I love your stories and the way you tell them. And what's the third point?

My third point is that I don't think I could become a psychologist.

Why is that?

I would have to be less judgmental of people.

Do you see yourself as judgmental? In what way?

Yes. And I have been judging people when they didn't accept my wishes to end my life.

That is certainly understandable. And I'm sure you understand that nobody who knows you would want to let you go.

I do understand that and I shouldn't really judge them, but I still do.

Well, we all judge one another. But you are right about letting go of judgment to be effective at psychotherapy. It's something I have to be alert to all the time. I'm sure I have been judgmental of you from time to time.

Oh really? About what?

Hmm. Well, sometimes, the thought of someone with your talent and abilities and so many people who love you, and just wanting to pack up and check out just seems a bit selfish.

Yes, but I'm not who I was before the stroke, so I'm not really being selfish.

I know you're not selfish. After all, you were worried about how ending your life would affect me and my practice. That's anything but selfish.

Anyway, I think this is why I cannot become a psychotherapist. I don't see myself becoming less judgmental.

Can you give me an example in your life of what you mean by being judgmental?

I remember being very judgmental toward my brother, Sudhanvshu. I didn't speak to him for about four years.

Oh, what happened?

He had moved here and lived here for quite a while. Then he decided to get married. He put an ad in the Indian American paper and found a woman of the same caste. Her name was Madhavi. After he met her, he went back to India and met some other Indian girls, but he came back and decided to marry Madhavi. She was from North Carolina.

His wedding was a delight. My other brother, Avinash, came from India. Joe came from Germany. Joe and I were the groom's parents at the wedding. But something changed after the wedding.

My brother started doing some strange things. He started bringing his old girlfriend into the home. When the old girlfriend was around, he was cheerful, and when the girlfriend was not around, he was not cheerful and became noncommunicative.

But, I didn't find out all this was going on until he asked his wife to leave. Madhavi came and stayed with me for a few weeks, and over the course of that time, she told me all about what had been going on.

I had a conversation with Sudhanvshu about what was going on. He said he had spoken to his lawyer and wanted to annul the marriage. I asked him about his behavior and he got very upset with me. He implied that his marital troubles were somehow my fault. He told me that he got married because *I* wanted him to get married.

I told him I didn't care if he was married. I wasn't married either. He said that I wanted him to marry because I couldn't marry. But he misunderstood something I said to him. I had told him that our mother said if you are going to get married then you should do it while you are young so you have the energy to raise the children.

He was determined to annul the marriage, so my friend Dia came and took Madhavi to live at her place. He was upset about that as well and we stopped talking for about four years. My friend Ed was also Sudhanvshu's friend and he kept in touch with him and let me know he was okay.

And you think that you were being judgmental of your brother?

I was judgmental about his choices and his behavior. I wasn't happy about what happened and I let four years go by not speaking to him. It was one time I really failed to be the Gay Crow.

But then you reconciled with him after the four years?

Yes, in fact, Sudhanvshu joined our company in 2000. And we have been on good terms since then. In 2009, he married a second time to an Indian woman. Joe and I went to India for the wedding. His second wife and their daughter are wonderful.

We've all got situations and people in our lives where we fail to live up to our own standards. We judge others and we judge ourselves and it is usually based on some kind of misunderstanding. I'm not sure that level of judgment disqualifies you from being a therapist.

As I read the book, that thought kept recurring for me that it would be difficult not to judge people.

Well, it is difficult not to judge people. Rogers is setting out a high standard there.

Yes. And I see in myself how it can affect people. When I first started coming to you, nobody seemed to understand my point about wanting to end my life. And that made me more determined to make you and others understand it.

But after the cruise, when I asked Joe again to let me go and he agreed to let me go, something changed for me. And others have now seen me and accepted that this is my choice. The more people accept me wanting to kill myself, the less I want to do it.

Wow. That is what Carl Rogers calls "the relational paradox." The more we are accepted as we are, the more willing we are to consider making changes. We want to be known and accepted and unencumbered by guilt or obligation.

Yes. I thought about that while I was reading *On Becoming a Person*.

I've been thinking a lot this week about what you said about how you inoculated yourself against many things, but not against a stroke, which you described as half-death.

Yes. Half-death seems a very good description of what it is like after the stroke.

And, you were telling me about how you were able to prepare yourself for death by disassociating or letting go of people and things. But you couldn't disassociate from Joe.

That's right.

And, you said you didn't know how to inoculate for the stroke because it was like half-death. But maybe inoculation isn't the

answer. Perhaps you need to disassociate from some things. But not *all* things as when you thought you were dying. Maybe couldn't you disassociate from some of the things in life, but not all of it?

Those times I disassociated from things and people like back in 2006, I was preparing to die. Death seemed inevitable and imminent.

And then you didn't die. And then you had to reassociate again. And did you find yourself making any new choices at that time? Did you choose not to reassociate with anything or anyone from your past?

Not really, but I reassociated with some old interests that I had let go of. Like painting.

You started painting again. You had been artistic in your youth as I recall.

Yes. I was interested in art from a young age. But I let go of it mostly before college. Back before the lymphoma, I started going to a group of amateur artists that would draw nude male models. The group was designed for gay men. I stopped my involvement after the lymphoma and the ankle accident. The group eventually stopped for other reasons.

Then in 2012, two men started a painting group again in a private space. It had the same idea, but it became a social group in addition to the drawing group. I met some very talented models there.

In December of 2013, one of the guys in the drawing group invited me to Alexandria to a class he was attending. It was a painting class. The class was taught by Rob Vander Zee, who was a famous artist. He conducted the class unlike the usual class, but more like a group experience. Each student brought his/her own painting that they were working on and Rob provided guidance and critique. I liked the format, so I joined the group.

In the first session, I drew a full-size figure of a nude man. It came out very nicely. So, I decided to try my hand at painting. My first painting was a nude I had drawn before in my drawing group. The group had a mixture of people that included some famous painters. There was one student, Jack, who was the owner of a gallery in DC. He was so impressed by the painting that he said, "If you do a series of such paintings, I will show them in my gallery." Excited, I started doing a series of such paintings.

By August 2014, I had twenty-one paintings. My aim was not to paint the skin tones but instead have each painting using the color of the emotion brought out by the painting. Jack loved it. He decided to have that whole series in his gallery. The art show was to open on October 18 for six weeks.

We decided to call it "The Male Spectrum." Jack wrote a beautiful description of my paintings for the show. He acknowledged my unique use of color to express emotion and he called the paintings lush and sensual. He said my painting style was captivating and compelling as well as comforting.

The show was a huge success. But it almost didn't happen. Two days before the opening, Jack was supposed to come over to my place to look at a couple of paintings, but he didn't show up. Then a couple days later, we heard that he had a heart attack and died.

So, his memorial service was held in the gallery with my paintings on display. The memorial was beautiful with a dancer, and music, and my artwork. Jack's partner said Jack was so happy about my show that it was very appropriate to have his memorial this way.

The opening was delayed and I think people who attended Jack's memorial were hesitant to attend for that reason. But otherwise, it was well-attended and people really enjoyed it.

Vishwas and Joe at "The Male Spectrum" exhibit, 2014

It sounds like yet another example of your endless capacity to take on a challenge. When I think of all the spheres of knowledge you have tackled, I'm simply amazed. You learned painting, poetry, and music. Engineering, of course, and artificial intelligence.

And sign language.

And how to be a gay man coming from a culture that didn't have gay on its radar. And how to get treatment for HIV when there was no treatment. And I know there are many other areas you have mastered.

But those all happened before my stroke.

That's true, but I have to believe you are underestimating your abilities. The common thread of all of those challenges is that you were in the thick of them with all your curiosity and your Gay Crow outlook. Now you are in a new challenge called, "Living with the Effects of a Stroke."

Maybe I'm just grieving my losses. One of the books talked about grief makes some people want to separate from everyone and everything.

Amazing. You're already thinking like a therapist.

I think I may have been adjusting like I did when I was dying. I adjusted by letting go.

No doubt. Maybe you don't want to become a therapist, and that's not what matters to me, but I think you have what it takes. Here's a thought experiment. Imagine you were a therapist and someone came in having had a stroke and looking for a reason to live or a new zest for life, what would you say to them?

Find a therapist you like and trust. Someone you can relate to, and find someone engaging. And the rest will take care of itself.

Good. What else might you say?

I would say, trust the process.

Vishwas, your gifts and genius extend far beyond your intelligence. In my field, they say good therapy heals both the client and the therapist. I want you to know that I've learned so much from being with you so far.

What have you learned?

I am never more aware of my own mortality and the fact that death is a part of life as when I am with you. A while back, when you told me about Vishwas 3.0, I saw a spark of that zest you have been looking for. I know you still feel like a part of you is gone since the stroke. And that may be true, but what is left is extraordinary.

Thank you.

I don't know if I can ever be quite the Gay Crow as you are, but you continue to teach me that I have a choice in how I see things and react to life.

I'm very happy that I could give back to you in that way. By the way, you keep telling me to write my memoirs. I really think *you* should write a book about your life and work. You could even use me as the subject!

Ha-ha! And I hope you decide to keep coming. We can talk about psychology until the cows come home. Maybe you'll decide to become a therapist or maybe you'll discover what there is to discover and lose interest.

That's what usually happens. Once I learn how something works, I lose interest.

But we will continue to learn from each other.

I would like that.

And let's agree about one thing.

What is that?

That original issue that you came in here for...the one that you say you put on the shelf for now while you continue to recover from your stroke.

What about it?

Now that's on you.

I agree. That's on me.

Thank you.

Now, what's the next psychology book?

Take your pick.

Epilogue

Life goes on and Joe and I went on more cruises. Our Alaskan cruise in 2018 was such a great experience. We saw icebergs and all kinds of birds and sea creatures. We continued onto the Canadian Mountaineer Railroad from Vancouver to Calgary. I was still in a wheelchair, but it was beautiful, fun, and full of great memories. Then in 2019, we went to Cancun on a two-week vacation, and in 2020, we went to Hawaii, New Zealand, and Australia.

I'm still recovering from my stroke little by little. Joe and I have a good life together. We love our friends and see them often.

I finally wrote this memoir after Carl, Joe, and so many others encouraged me. I didn't really want the book to be about my stroke but about my wonderful life up to that time. I was working with a ghostwriter, Max J. Miller, during the pandemic of 2020–2021 and he suggested that framing my story as a dialogue with my therapist, Carl, would be a compelling way to tell the story. We took some poetic license in how those discussions actually went, but the content is all true and faithful to our time together.

After my stroke, finding Carl was itself a "stroke" of fortune. He is the best person I have met in years. He was always open and honest with me. I needed a friend at that time. I needed intellectual stimulation and engagement. I needed a new challenge in life. He provided all of that.

We met weekly for about a year. It took about six months for me to get to the place where I was no longer thinking about ending my life. By then, the subject of psychology and therapy had become my new puzzle to solve. We continued to meet weekly for another year or so. Then we began meeting only once a month for a while.

Eventually, I was able to embrace that the continuities of my life were at least equal to the discontinuities before and after my stroke. Of all the things I am grateful to Carl for, perhaps the most significant is the recognition that I am still and will always be the Gay Crow.

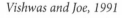

Vishwas and Joe, 1991   *Joe and Vishwas, 2021*

Appendix:
Vishwas' Poetry

भोंदू

त्वा काय कराव्या फुका जगाच्या
कल्याणाच्या बाता, असता
अन्धाराच्या खोल खोल गर्तेत
बुडाला स्वतः
वृथा तू काय देखिले दुखा, वृता तू
काया भोगिले सुखा,
मुखावर कोठवरी पांघरून फिरशील
वैरागी बूरखा

Hypocrite

You give false advice about
doing good, yet you are in
the dark.
You have not experienced
happiness, nor have you
known sorrow.
How long will you go
around with this false claim
of being a sage?

जाणिवेचा क्षण

कधी भासतो मी मज दुजा
 खचितच नच हा मी, मज माझा
देह सोडूनी कोणी वदतो
 कळते मज मी कोण, कोण तो
तरी मी मजसी म्हणतो माझा
 आणि निसटतो क्षण जाणिवेचा

~

 कधी साद तो आतून घालून
 म्हणतो मज ये, मजसी सोडून
 कळते मज, मज हेच हवे ते
 परी काहीसे मागे अडते
 हून मी घेतो कौल मनाचा
 आणि निसटतो क्षण जाणिवेचा

~

कधी शोध मी त्याचा घेता
 फिरतो गर गर चक्री पुरता
थकतो, हरतो, नाद सोडतो
 मना अस्तित्वा रमण्या बघतो
गृहितची धरतो अर्थ जिण्याचा
 आणि निसटतो क्षण जाणिवेचा

The Moment of Realization

Sometimes it seems like I'm someone else. "This is not me," says someone other than me. I realize that's what I want. But I call myself "me," and I miss the moment of realization.

Sometimes, he calls me from inside myself. "Leave yourself and come to me," he says. I know that's what I want. But I check myself for validation, and I miss the moment of realization.

Sometimes I search for him. I look for him until I get dizzy. I give up. I try to enjoy life as it is, and I miss the moment of realization.

152

पसारा

नव्हता तेव्हा काळ सुद्धा जेव्हा मी
केले सुरु
  कण कण सांधयाला अन् दिशा
दश बांधयाला

लय, नाद, शब्द, ब्रह्म, विश्व, मित्र,
शशी, धरा
  केले मीच निर्माण मिथ्या, सत्य
आत्मा गुन्तायाला

जीव, जंतु, जीवन, मृत्यु, मोह,
माया सारे खरे
  खरे भासण्या इतके दिले नियम
आखून विज्ञान पुरे

ठेवली होती वाट एक यातुनी मी
बाहेर पुरी
  कुठे, कशी, काही केल्या आठवत
नाही आता मुळी

कुणास ठाऊक कशासाठी केला मी
हा खटाटोप सारा
  गुंतुन पडलोय स्वतःच आता
आवरत नाही हा पसारा

The Mess

When I started to build the
universe, even the concept of
time didn't exist.

From then on, I started building the atoms and molecules
and giving the dimensions.
From there, I created the
world, the sun, the moon,
and the universe for the real
soul to be in. I created life
and death, the attraction, and
the repellant, all with a set of
guiding science.

I had left an escape route out
of this, but somehow I can't
find it.

Why did I create this mess?
I cannot get hold of this anymore.

नेती नेती

जीवन चक्रे भोगू अशी किती
   सुख दुःखाचे कण घोळू किती
अणू गर्भांचे गर्भ करु किती
   वाट अनंताचि पाहू किती
किती विस्तारु ज्ञानाच्या मिती
   किती धुंडाळू काळाच्या क्षिती
माहित असुनी मजला अंती
   नेती नेती नेती नेती

Not That Not That

How long should I live
through cycles of life and
death?

How long should I experi-
ence happiness and sorrow?

How much do I split the
atoms?

How much do I expand the
universe?

How much do I expand the
knowledge?

How much do I expand the
limits of time and dimension?

When I know that ultimately
the answer is nothingness.

Not that Not that Not that
Not that.

मोक्ष

अदृश्याच्या अमूर्त आशयाला
मातीच्या मूर्तीत ओतणार्‍या

अनंताच्या अंतिम जाणिवेला
भूमितीच्या भौतिकात रेखणार्‍या

ओम्काराच्या आदी नादाला अन्
ब्रह्माच्या वैदिक लयीला
संगिताच्या सात सूरांमधे शोधणार्‍या

काव्याच्या विशुद्ध संवेदनेला
कवितेच्या कोशात जखडणार्‍या

आत्माची अमर्याद उर्जा सोडून
इंधनासाठी धरा खोदणार्‍या

अंतरातील अंतास अंतरून
मुक्तीचा मार्ग मागणार्‍या

माझ्या अजाण मनास कोणी सांगेल का
की ब्रह्माने ब्रह्माला ब्रह्मात शोधायचे
सोडून

ब्रह्म ब्रह्मातील अद्वैत जाणले
तर मुक्ताला मुक्त मोक्ष मिळेल

Freedom

My mind which tries to
find the meaning in the
unknown,

the one who tries to
measure the infinite with
trigonometry,

the one who tries to find
the emptiness in music,

the one who finds energy
in fossils while ignoring
the energy in the universes,

the one who is trying to
find the realization in
worldly things,

Would someone explain
that freedom is in the mind
of the one who is already
free?

Appendix B

Vishwas's Stroke and Me
(Joe's Impressions)

On the twenty-ninth of January 2016, my partner of twenty-four years and husband of just under a year suffered a debilitating stroke while working out at our gym. I was at the gym at the time, but since our routines were different, I was not with him.

I had seen him briefly, but my workout that day was an hour on the treadmill while he was using the weight machines. When I finished my workout, I headed to the locker room for a shower. As I entered the locker room, Vishwas was exiting. He looked a little unsteady, and when I asked if he was alright, he replied that he was not feeling "right" and would see me at home. I went to shower. When I was finished, I headed out and saw Vishwas sitting in a chair near the door. He asked me to help him to his car because he was feeling shaky. As we exited the gym, I realized that he was having trouble walking and was not in the shape to drive. I asked him to lean against a pole for balance while I went for my car. We agreed that I would drive and we could retrieve his car later.

I knew that something was wrong, but I did not know what or how serious it was. I asked if he wanted to go to the emergency room and, at first, he said yes. A few seconds later, he said, "Let's just go home. Let me lie down for a while and see how I feel." I agreed. We got home and he walked into the house and straight back to the bedroom. I put away my gym gear. He was only in bed for a couple of minutes and then came into the living room. He seemed very anxious and a little confused. I said I would call our doctor. I was connected to the nurse and described what I was seeing. She asked me to look at his face and ask him to smile. When he tried to smile, I could see his face was drooping on the right side. The nurse told me to drive to the emergency room immediately. I knew then that he was having a stroke.

Fortunately, we do not live far from the hospital and got there very quickly. After that, things moved very fast. We were immediately checked through at the emergency department and taken to a treatment room. The ER doctor checked him, confirmed that he was having a stroke, and ordered a scan. He was taken right away, and when he returned, the doctor explained that they wanted to administer TPA, sometimes referred to as "a clot buster." Because they had determined that it was an ischemic stroke, they wanted to prevent further damage by breaking up the clot that was impeding blood flow. We agreed and he was wheeled out for that treatment.

My head was spinning and Vishwas was off for the TPA treatment. One of the nurses explained the purpose of the TPA. She indicated that that was all she could say at the time and left to attend to her other responsibilities. I was left alone with the awareness that the most important person in my life was about to face a dramatic change in his life. My first and only thought in that moment was, "And I will be with him."

Following the TPA, the next step was moving Vishwas to a room and getting him settled for the night. They told me that they would be watching him and running some tests in the morning. One of the doctors said that he would need a lot of therapy and we would have decisions to make. Then he said, "Without the TPA, he would not be going to therapy, but to life support." I thought to myself, "No way."

The rest of that day and night was a blur. I know I went home for clothes and stuff. There was a sofa that opened into a bed and we slept.

The next morning, medical personnel were in and out of the room. There was a neurologist who I believe looked in, did not say much (if anything), and later sent a bill. There were nurses and a woman who talked to us about rehab options. The choices came down to three: Inova, where we were, had no private rooms available; Mt. Vernon seemed too far to travel every day; and Virginia Hospital Center was manageable. We decided on VHC.

We really had no idea of what the time schedule was going to be and neither did any of the people we asked. It was a question of availability and logistics. I assumed that something would happen in the morning, but in the evening, we were told that we were ready to move. I had my car and said that I would follow the ambulance. Of course, that was a mistake because I had to park in a different lot. I did find my way eventually, but it all seemed rather strange. As far as I could tell, it was just a matter of getting him into the room and nothing was going to happen until the next morning.

What I remember about rehab, which lasted a month, was sleeping in a hospital room, watching Vishwas struggle to get his bearings, struggle to move, and try to make sense of an unimaginable reality. What I felt was helpless.

My memories of that month are a little disordered. It is difficult to keep track of time when you are not even sure what day it is. The stroke had affected his right side, which was his dominant side.

We knew that rehab was going to be intense. The hardest thing for Vishwas and for me was discovering the extent of his limitations.

Rehab had three components: Physical therapy, which we discovered was mostly concerned with the lower body (primarily legs). Occupational therapy was about doing things like getting dressed and showering. The third component was speech pathology. One of the effects of the stroke was that Vishwas was not always able to find the right words to express himself. Eventually, I was able to translate his thoughts by context. Over time, this problem resolved itself as his speech improved.

After a full month of inpatient rehab, Vishwas was discharged and returned home. We arranged for in-home therapy and began sessions with a physical therapist, Willberto. Compatibility, as we dis-

covered, is an essential element in therapy, and Vishwas and Willberto worked well together. In this period, progress was slow, but steady.
We had gotten used to the refrain "Every stroke is different," which
was the answer to every question. "How long will this take?" "Every
stroke is different." "Am I where I should be at this point?" "Every
stroke is different?" We got the message, but of course, we wanted
to see more progress. It was much harder on Vishwas than for me.
He was the "stroke survivor;" I was an observer. In general, I think I
was more aware of progress than he was, but despite his frustration,
he continued to work hard. Throughout the whole process, my sense
of time became less and less accurate. I think the at-home therapy
continued for a couple of months. Next, we started therapy at the
local hospital on an outpatient basis. The therapy sessions there were
good, but not always consistent. It was a slow process.

Six months after the stroke, Vishwas was doing okay. He was dili-
gent (most of the time) about his exercises and doing whatever he
could. Then, he suffered the biggest setback in the recovery process—he had a fall. He had been getting around in the house with
a four-pronged cane and was becoming somewhat confident. How
or why the fall occurred was never really clear, but the result was
devastating. His face and jaw were damaged. He had to have ex-
tensive dental work done including realignment of his teeth. The
worst effect, in terms of recovery, was that his left wrist was broken.
For the next two months, he was unable to use his left hand. As his
right side was still paralyzed, this seriously limited his movements.
I believe this event and the consequent circumstances led him to
question the value of going on.

He was reevaluating his life. He had done well, was successful, and despite life-threatening illnesses, a few broken bones, and predictions by medical experts that he would not survive very long, he was here thirty years later and had been mostly happy. He told me what he was thinking and why. It made sense to me on an intellectual level; emotionally it was a different thing altogether. There was a sense that he had been living on borrowed time for decades and was reluctant to take out another loan. Maybe, this was enough. He had come to a decision. It was a good time to exit on his own terms.

What followed might have surprised most people, but did not surprise me. He continued to work at his therapy. We traveled. We saw friends and family. He smiled and laughed. With most people, he was his usual self. It was not a pretense. He shared his thought process and his decision with a few close friends. I had the conviction in my mind and in my heart that this man whom I knew and loved was, above all, a survivor. It took some time and some struggle to understand that in some way even if he followed through on his decision, that too would be survival. I gave him what I could, not advice but my thoughts and feelings. I did not want him to go. I would grieve and I would miss him. I was tempted to be selfish, to insist that he change his mind. I loved him too much for that. So, I told him, "I will be here for you in every way I can, but I will accept your choice, because it is yours to make."

I did ask him if he was willing to talk to a therapist or counselor for a second opinion. He agreed and went online to "shop around." He met with two different therapists who were not a good fit, but on the third try, he found a therapist who understood where he was coming from. The therapeutic relationship grew into a friendship, which Vishwas continues to treasure, as do I. His therapist encouraged him to tell his story, which resulted in his book, *Gay Crow*.

The stroke changed his life and to a lesser extent mine. Our circumstances are altered, but the fundamentals are still in place. Vishwas is the man I met, was attracted to, and came to know. I fell in love with him. It was the best thing that I have ever done. We continue to live our lives, have had great adventures, incredible vacations, and good times with wonderful friends. Our families are accepting and loving to both of us. For the most part, things are good. There is much more that I could say, but this is enough.

I used to wonder, while in this relationship with this amazing person, what does a guy like me bring to the table. What do I have to offer? I don't wonder about that anymore. I have an answer. It is three simple words, "I am here." I think that is what he needs from me and what he will always have.